What's most impressive is Bernadette Stankard's practical applications of lessons and activities for each type of intelligence, which builds a young person's faith in a unique way. *How Each Child Learns* respects and celebrates the God-given differences in each human being.

> Brad Grabs, teacher, Rockhurst High School,
> Kansas City, Kansas

What a pleasant book to read and have in one's personal library. I strongly urge and recommend that religious educators take advantage of this exceptionally well-written book.

> Oliver Manungo, Harare, Zimbabwe, teacher

By using multiple intelligences techniques, our catechists are able to get students actively engaged in learning about their faith and understanding it in their hearts as well as their heads. Thanks to Bernadette Stankard for teaching us so many ways to share the message of Jesus.

> Father John Brungardt, Chancellor,
> Catholic Diocese of Wichita

Our religious education and youth leaders left the retreat (based on the principles in *How Each Child Learns*) with a renewed fire in their hearts for the gospel and a deeper commitment to their own prayer life and of how they can help catechists experience prayer through the insights of multiple intelligences.

> Joe Streett, Director of Religious Education,
> Diocese of Erie

In *How Each Child Learns*, Stankard empowers the reader to discover and use his or her own gifts by encouraging the gifts of others. In a very accessible style, she provides practical and fun exercises for drawing out the innate intelligences in every child.

> Amy Viets, Children's Ministry Director,
> Holy Cross Lutheran Church, Overland Park, Kansas

HOW
EACH CHILD
Learns

Using Multiple Intelligence in Faith Formation

Bernadette T. Stankard

Second printing 2007

Twenty-Third Publications
A Division of Bayard
One Montauk Avenue, Suite 200
P.O. Box 6015
New London, CT 06320
(860) 437-3012 or (800) 321-0411
www.23rdpublications.com
ISBN 978-1-58595-269-4

The Scripture passages contained herin are from the *New Revised Standard Version of the Bible*, copyright© 1989, by the Division of christian Education of the National Council of Churches in the U.S.A. All rights reserved.

Library of Congress Catalog Card Number: 2003104396
Printed in the U.S.A.

Contents

Introduction   1

CHAPTER I
The Theory of Multiple Intelligence   7

CHAPTER II
Verbal-Linguistic   15

CHAPTER III
Logical-Mathematical   27

CHAPTER IV
Musical-Rhythmic   40

CHAPTER V
Visual-Spatial   49

CHAPTER VI
Bodily-Kinesthetic   57

CHAPTER VII
Naturalist   66

CHAPTER VIII
Intrapersonal   76

CHAPTER IX
Interpersonal   88

CHAPTER X
Existential   96

CHAPTER XI
Let's Get Specific   104

CHAPTER XII
Taking a Leap   109

Resources   113

Introduction

Very truly, I tell you, when you were younger, you used to fasten your own belt and to go wherever you wished. But when you grow old, you will stretch out your hands, and someone else will fasten a belt around you and take you where you do not wish to go.
                                                                    John 21:18

Bill Peet, noted children's writer, tells the story of a horse named Clyde, who was such a coward he didn't want to accompany his knight, Sir Galavant, into battle against the dragons of the world. Clyde was desperate to keep anyone from seeing his fear, so he spent his entire life trying to avoid situations that would call for bravery. Unfortunately for Clyde, one day, Sir Galavant heard of an ogre terrorizing a nearby village, and the knight insisted that he and Clyde go to slay the beast. Clyde had no choice but to accompany his knight.

They found the ogre deep in the forest sleeping. Clyde breathed a sigh of relief, thinking that they could easily slay the beast and be on their way before he woke up. Sir Galavant had other ideas. He wanted a fair fight so he woke the ogre and the battle began.

Clyde, filled with terror, saw his master had no hope of winning so he turned and headed at a fast gallop out of the forest despite the protests of Sir Galavant. In the horse's panic, he didn't notice a low hanging tree

1

branch, which knocked Sir Galavant off the horse's back. Clyde arrived outside of the forest to find his master missing and quickly surmised what had happened. Despite his chattering teeth and shaking knees, Clyde summoned up all his courage to go back and try to save his master.

Clyde found the ogre toying with Sir Galavant, building up his appetite before eating him. Slowly Clyde crept up and with all his might bit the ogre's tail. Angered, the ogre chased after Clyde, who ran for his life. The ogre tightened the distance and finally caught the horse's tail. Clyde, with his last ounce of strength, pulled the ogre out into the sunlight.

Of course, anyone who knows anything about ogres knows they are afraid of sunlight. The ogre looked around terrified, then screamed and disappeared. Happily, Sir Galavant and Clyde carried the good news to the villagers. Clyde felt very brave indeed. His world had changed, he had grown stronger, and, in the words of Bill Peet, "after all, a horse who bites a giant ogre on the tail and lives to trot another day is just about as brave as anyone can be."

Our growth in religious education is much like Clyde's journey. We are good at what we do. We cover the material. We get the job done. Deep down, however, we are scared of taking the leap of courage that can bring us to a new level of awareness. Sometimes the fear is so great that we don't enter the forest. We stay hovering at the edge, waiting for someone else to take the plunge into the trees. Sometimes the fear takes the form of a patrol, discouraging anyone else from entering that forest, from making any change.

Tolbert McCarroll, in his book *Guiding God's Children*, wrote,

I have been associated with a large number of people who are seriously frustrated in their adult spiritual quests because they have been deprived of an appropriate spiritual formation in their childhood. They live in a painful tension and often find release in non-constructive and shallow experiences. Some are flexible enough to become as little children again and to have a new start, even quite late in life. But many are not able to do so, and they continue to build elaborate superstructures without any foundation. Time after time their castles fall down.

Many of us have been deprived of the appropriate spiritual formation that, as McCarroll points out, enables us to experience God and experience growth. So many of us want to stay like Clyde, pretending to be brave without having to be brave, pretending to believe without having to believe. We want to raise our children to believe, but we can be fearful of the challenges involved in that process. Something has to change. Christ is calling us to raise our children and ourselves in such a way that we go into the forest despite our fear and discover the beauty of God within us.

The multiple intelligence theory is a great way to take the leap of courage that faith demands. The theory enables us to reach beyond what we were taught, to reach beyond the box we often put God in, to touch each other in a way that makes every encounter pregnant with the Spirit.

When I first started using multiple intelligences in the classroom, I would leave each encounter amazed at what had surfaced as a result of taking the leaps of faith required in trying something new. Granted, the changes were not easy to make. More than once I thought I would be run out of town on a rail, or I convinced myself I was never going into a classroom again. But the children and the adults responded in a way that told me I was dabbling in something that promised great results.

This feeling was further enforced during catechetical gatherings. When I attended conferences or training sessions, it amazed me to hear a speaker talk as if he or she knew God personally, knew what God was and was not capable of doing, and ruled on whether or not God would or would not like something. I was always uncomfortable with that approach. Gradually I came to realize that my discomfort sprang from the fact that these people were boxing God into a way of behaving they felt comfortable with. It had nothing to do with who God was. It had everything to do with how willing individuals were to stretch their faith.

Unboxing my thinking and teaching about God has become paramount for me. We don't know God. Sure, we know bits and pieces as God has been revealed to us over the ages—but we don't know enough to speak definitively about who God is. Besides, it always seems that as soon as I think I know God, something happens to show me that I don't know as much as I thought I did.

Using multiple intelligences in religion classes and in my own spiritual life enables me to keep God out of the box. When I was singing the story of the woman at the well, I was learning how her spirit rose and fell as she spoke with Jesus. When I was pretending to be the towel that washed the feet of the apostles at the Last Supper, I was learning the difficulty of being a servant. When I compared peanut butter to God, I learned what it was to be crushed and given over to make something that nourished another.

Multiple intelligences speak to the character of God. When my daughter came home from preschool one day and announced that God made the world magic, that there were surprises everywhere, I realized how profound her statement was. God is full of surprises. God is the God of humor, the God of dance, the God of suffering, the God of clichés, the God of creativity, the God of boredom, the God of pain, the God of dirt, the God of flowers. God is so varied we can't even come close to comprehending God in full. Multiple intelligences give us a small glimpse into that fullness. Using multiple intelligences, God is the God of words, the God of rhythm, the God of logic, the God of movement, the God of community, the God of personhood, the God of art, the God of questions and answers—and more.

A story by Daniel Juniper in his book, *Along the Water's Edge*, tells of the puddle fish. Day after day these fish swam in circles and fought one another for water bugs. One day a beautiful rainbow fish landed in their puddle and spoke about the sea, the place that fish were meant for. When the other fish asked how to get there, the sparkling fish told them that they had to swim to the edge of their puddle, jump into the river, and trust that the river would carry them into the sea.

Fish after fish presented reasons why they couldn't make that leap. After all, they knew the truth. Finally, the rainbow fish told them they had to make a decision because spring was coming and the puddle would soon dry up. The sparkling fish invited them once again to take the leap. Only a few joined the sparkling fish. Together they jumped into the river, and the current swept them away to the sea.

The remaining puddle fish were quiet for a long time, and then they resumed swimming in circles and fighting for water bugs.

If we aren't careful, we can become like the puddle fish, keeping God in that puddle, never taking the leap into the river, never being carried to the sea, the place that fish were meant for. When we unbox our approach to God, when we use multiple intelligences to take a leap toward the sea, we open possibilities and we open ourselves to God's surprises.

D. H. Lawrence wrote, "Acknowledge the wonder." With multiple intelligences we can acknowledge the wonder of God and have a great time doing so. Turn the page for the beginning of the adventure.

CHAPTER I

The Theory of Multiple Intelligence

Now there are varieties of gifts, but the same Spirit; and there are varieties of services, but the same Lord; and there are varieties of activities, but it is the same God who activates all of them in everyone. To each is given the manifestation of the Spirit for the common good.

1 Corinthians 12:4–7

Sometimes a mother just knows. And with my daughter, I just knew. She was very intelligent, quick with comparisons, filled with knowledge, and she created things at the drop of a hat. She had gifts which, at the age of seven, were only beginning to surface. Unfortunately, the school district didn't know what I knew.

It all began with standardized testing. During the first test, Petra outshone her fellow classmates; in the second, she wallowed at slightly below average. Test after test proved to be following the same schizoid path. The bottom line was the district's decision that she did not qualify to participate in the gifted program.

Neither I nor my husband was willing to stand by and watch her fall through the cracks and perhaps see her learn to hate learning. After much discussion and soul searching, we proposed to the district an alternative program for Petra and those like her. The program would follow the same guidelines as the district's gifted program: one day away from the regular classroom, no penalty for missed daily work, and ample opportunities for enrichment.

The Spirit works in mysterious ways. I found myself, a person not trained in education, in the classroom in charge of a group of children who from the very first day kept me learning and growing. The classroom included anywhere between two and ten children, in the second through sixth grades. One of the children struggled with attention deficit disorder, while another was diagnosed with bi-polar disorder.

I can't say everything went smoothly. We had our good days and our bad days but overall, I came away each day with a feeling that good things were happening. The student with ADD was now able to concentrate on an activity for up to an hour or more. The child with the bi-polar disorder was able to learn how to better work in conjunction with others. The others looked forward to coming to the classroom because, as one of the boys put it, "I can do so much in here, much more than in my regular class. I can't learn enough."

The classroom, while nurturing the individual interests of the students—studying the anatomy of a cow's heart, building structures out of straws, running a courtroom, making animated films—created a natural outgrowth of community, not only among themselves but with the total school. Once each semester, the students gave a school-wide presentation where all kindergarten through sixth grade students came and experienced a topic. The rainforest experience was the most popular—it included a taste of Ben and Jerry's Rainforest Crunch ice cream—because the children were able to sing, make things, dance, imagine, and think.

My daughter went on to college to pursue studies in religion and education. She excelled in debate and Spanish, biology and drama, music and history, peer mediation and leadership. I am convinced the experience she had during her grade school years which enabled her to learn in the ways she knew best, contributed in large part to her present success both as a student and a person. The other students in that enhanced learning class tell of similar achievements, as do the parents who implemented these ideas at home.

This was the beginning of my trip into multiple intelligences.

Meet Howard Gardner

Back in 1983, Howard Gardner, professor of education at Harvard University, postulated that the traditional notion of intelligence based on IQ testing was very limited. He felt educators were only addressing two of the intelligence through which people learn: verbal-linguistic and logical-mathematical.

Gardner believed "intelligence is the ability to find and solve problems, and create products of value in one's own culture." Therefore, he began scientific research and came up with several intelligence, ways in which people learn and in which they present their unique gifts. The theory of multiple intelligence shook the educational community, a community that had become very comfortable with the notion that intelligence was a genetic, measurable quality. Each intelligence went through rigorous testing before it qualified as a recognized intelligence through which people learn. Extensive research composed of interviews, tests, and investigation of hundreds of individuals took place. Gardner studied stroke and accident victims, prodigies, autistic individuals, those with learning disabilities, idiot savants, and people from diverse cultures.

Gardner has never questioned the existence of a general intelligence; rather, he points to intelligence not covered by one concept. He argues that intelligence is centered in many different areas of the brain and that each of those intelligence are interconnected; they rely on each other and yet can operate independently.

Gardner stressed that although individuals might have one strong intelligence through which they initially take in information, each person has all the intelligence to some degree, and all the intelligence act in collaboration with one another. This theory, unlike the original I.Q. theory which excluded certain individuals, allows everyone to learn according to their own strengths, a revolutionary approach that emphasizes the unique gifts and talents of each individual.

As I learned more and more about the theory of multiple intelligence, I began to think of how it could be helpful in the religious education setting. My first opportunity to test my thoughts came when I made a presentation to a group of religious educators in my diocese.

Anyone who has done any program presentations knows teachers can be a difficult audience. Not only do they sometimes approach the experience with an attitude of "I could be doing something else," they often come to the presentation with the feeling that there is nothing new under the sun. And there I was, someone with little background in teaching, attempting to tell them they could energize their teaching through the use of multiple intelligences.

The presentation started easily enough. I talked about the theory and about the different intelligence. But then I realized that the very thing I had wanted to avoid was happening: I had lost the teachers. Some were correcting papers, some were paging through their books, others were simply staring off into space. Then the Spirit nudged me. "Do something," it said. "Show them how it works."

I was flabbergasted. Of course I had done many multiple intelligence exercises in the enhanced learning classroom, but never in the religious education classroom. What could I do to communicate the importance of using multiple intelligence in religion classes? At this point, I remember whispering a prayer: "Okay, God. It's all in your hands now." The parable of the sower and the seed floated through my head. I would use this story to show the intelligence at work.

And so we read the story from the Bible. We acted it out. We sang about it. We had the sower meet the seeds. We talked about what it meant to us to hear this story. We imagined what a field might be like with the rocks and poor soil and the birds. We calculated how many seeds might be in the sower's bag. We listed all the participants in the story. And we each paired up with our special seed.

I can't say it was my greatest hour as a presenter, but I was able to demonstrate the theory of multiple intelligence to the religious educators far better than I could have ever done just by talking. We experienced the gospel story in the intelligences present in that room, and no one walked away without feeling that they had been touched. Through the guidance of the Spirit I had taught them about the sower in ways they had not experienced before. God was alive, and God's magic was afoot in the classroom that day.

What makes the theory of multiple intelligence so great is the way it provides many different paths to learning. If a catechist is having difficulty communicating an idea through the normal approaches of verbal-linguistic or logical-mathematical, he or she can fall back on one of the other intelligences to communicate the idea.

With multiple intelligence you can use words (verbal-linguistic) or numbers (logical-mathematical) or pictures (visual-spatial). You might use music (musical) or self-reflection (intrapersonal) or dance (bodily-kinesthetic). You can have a social encounter (interpersonal) or use whatever natural resources are at hand (naturalistic). Or you might sit back and ponder what it is all about (existential). All of these ways help us learn, and one or more of these ways helps each person learn best. You might liken this truth to the keys to the kingdom. Once you have the right key, the way in is easily secured. Once you have identified your strongest intelligence, the door to learning and growth is opened.

I continued along my path, gradually learning more about ways to use multiple intelligences in the classroom, and more specifically, in the religious education classroom. A turning point in this process came unexpectedly.

I was working with my preschool religious education class of ten three- and four-year-olds who were busy working around the room. I felt confident that I was addressing their needs, and most importantly, addressing each of their major intelligences. One little boy, however, seemed to be having difficulty staying on track. He was obviously verbal-linguistic, and he loved to talk and tell stories. He even attempted to write books with the few words he knew how to spell.

This day, the boy was busy putting words to a timeline about the announcement of Jesus' birth. Normally, this would have been a good exercise for him; yet he was in the midst of trying to make the word cards into paper airplanes and placing them in various formations across the sequence picture.

"Michael, what are you up to?" I asked in my most formal teacher voice.

"Nafin'." He pushed a paper airplane around on the picture.

"Have you matched up the words?" I looked at the pictures. "Remember, the words tell about the pictures."

He pulled at my sleeve and let out the longest sigh I had ever heard.

"Don't you know I'm more than words?"

Nothing else could have brought home that important lesson more clearly. I had fallen into the pitfall of so many teachers: I had labeled my children. Michael was no longer Michael-intent-on-learning. Michael had become verbal-linguistic-intelligence-Michael, totally incapable of taking in information through any of his other intelligence. I was giving him only experiences in his strong intelligence, not challenging him beyond. He recognized this, and I needed him to point it out so that I would stop and think.

Responding to the Individual

Multiple intelligence is an approach to education that is designed to be responsive to individual cognitive differences. Gardner said it best when he stated, "Know as much as you can about the kids rather than make them pass through the same eye of the needle." When I zeroed in on Michael as verbal-linguistic, I began to feed him information only through this intelligence. Instead he needed to stretch his experience so that his intellect could develop to its fullest.

Gardner advocates the importance of helping students understand the concepts they are learning and of using the intelligence—*all* the intelligences—interactively to help individuals achieve understanding. That's what we are about in religious education, be it elementary, secondary, or adult. We are about helping people internalize their faith by engaging their whole person.

It has been many years since my first foray into the world of multiple intelligences. Since that time I have come to realize the beauty of God's creation through this theory. God makes us unique and yet connected. God calls us continually beyond ourselves, urging us to grow to become the best people we can be. God gifts us all and gives us many ways in which to know our Creator.

I once addressed a group of catechists and religious educators during a statewide conference. The room was packed. I had my notes. I knew where I was headed, but the moment I looked up at the group, I knew I couldn't go there. Instead I began to introduce myself using the multiple intelligence. I sang. I counted the letters in my name. I told the story of St. Bernadette. I talked about my sister's recent death. I took them on a genealogy tour which told them I was first generation American with deep roots in Poland. I shook hands with various individuals. I mused with them about the reasons why I was there to talk with them about religious education.

No one forgot my name and each individual in that room had an experience of learning that would not have happened if I had chosen a more "regular" route. We went on to act out parables, and see individuals from the Bible meet each other for the first time. We created cheers about God, prayed through a gamut of emotions using only the name

"Jesus," told elaborate stories, and shared our deepest faith encounters. At the end of the session I was delightfully tired and terrifically energized. I had experienced the faith of the community.

Because I was willing to take a risk and touch these individuals through their various intelligences, I was gifted by an experience of God I will never forget. The participants opened doors to aspects of God I hadn't thought about, portrayed people from the Bible in a new light, and showed me different ways to pray. In short, they had challenged my total being to grow.

That is what it is all about. Your total being needs to grow. The theory of multiple intelligence helps us meet that challenge and it is a challenge we need to extend to our children, to our young adults, and to our total community.

In the following pages we will look at the different intelligences and gain a deeper understanding of each of them. Since I am a person of practical leanings, I will include exercises that demonstrate the intelligences in religion class and faith formation gatherings. These are presented only as starting points. Ultimately, it's all about using your own intelligence. It's something called creativity—but that's another story.

Howard Gardner said, "If you want to teach something that's important, there's more than one way to teach it." What's more important for Christians than imparting our faith to others? We need to go beyond the way we have always taught our faith and move into the uncharted regions of the mind and spirit. Multiple intelligence will be a powerful guide on that journey.

CHAPTER II

Verbal-Linguistic

In the beginning was the Word, and the Word was with God, and the Word was God.

John 1:1

Okay; control the urge to move onto the next chapter. Because we have been most exposed to verbal-linguistic intelligence, we may feel we know it inside and out. Most of us have gone through years of education where verbal-linguistic intelligence was the primary means of receiving information. Lectures, presentations, papers, book reports, poems: we wrote, we read, we talked.

Because of this heavy emphasis on word skills, we also fell into a rut. When we thought of how to present material to one another, it came in the form of a book or a paper or a talk. When we wanted to communicate our knowledge, we resorted to the tried and true methods of communication. In short, we took this intelligence for granted.

Let's go back and look at the definition of verbal-linguistic intelligence. Gardner defines this intelligence as a sensitivity to the sounds, rhythms, and meaning of words, along with a sensitivity to different functions of language. Verbal-linguistic learners have highly developed auditory skills and enjoy reading and writing. Usually they enjoy word games and have a good memory for names and places. These people are the storytellers and the poets. Verbal-linguistic people like words for the sake of words.

My son has a highly developed linguistic intelligence. One of his favorite things is to roll certain words off his tongue. Macadamia. Blubber. Muck. Whereas most parents remember when their child walked or smiled or got their first tooth, I remember the time Nathaniel discovered the word "inconceivable." It rolled off his tongue and mine numerous times for days following. Learning new words was something that elated his soul. Verbal-linguistic learners share that passion.

Many school learning systems are based on verbal-linguistic intelligence because it is easy to measure. The knowledge of words can be tested, and the assimilation of information can be easily evaluated. In religious education classes, it is a welcome intelligence because it gives the catechist a tactile way to know if a child has assimilated the basics of Church teaching, sacrament preparation, and other key areas.

Although there are many advantages to using this approach, we have to be careful to remember that there are other ways of learning. I am reminded of a time when I worked in a parish in Northern Minnesota. Confirmation was approaching, and as part of the confirmation program individual interviews would be conducted with each of the teenagers. Part of the interview dealt with their "knowledge." Did they know enough about the sacrament to be confirmed? Did they know what the confirmation symbols were? Would the teens be able to answer any question the bishop should pose to them?

One young man came in for his interview, and began to work on the first part, a question and answer sheet regarding confirmation. When he was done, I went over the answers with him. He knew all the answers, and I congratulated him for his flawless paper. After this, we moved into the second part of the interview. We talked about his family and his friends. We talked about church and about how he felt about being confirmed. The more we talked, the more it became evident that this young man did not want the sacrament. In fact, he was feeling that he would be punished by God if, in his words, he "slapped God in the face by being confirmed and not believing."

Needless to say, following this interview I met with the young man and his parents, and together we decided to postpone his confirmation until he felt the Catholic faith was the faith he wanted to commit to.

In this case, the verbal-linguistic part of the test had told me one thing. The interpersonal part with the young man told quite a different story. If I had relied only on the linguistic part, I never would have known his feelings regarding the sacrament.

Verbal-linguistic intelligence is best taken in context. It is a powerful intelligence that carries the capability of painting strong word pictures that can move hearts and minds. It can also be detrimental when used poorly. When we address verbal-linguistic intelligence—actually this is true with every intelligence—we must look at all aspects of the intelligence. Thus, it is important to look at new ways of using the verbal-linguistic intelligence. Put aside the worksheets and the tests that simply record what facts a person knows. Put aside the reports on saints. Put aside working exclusively from the text. Use verbal-linguistic intelligence as every intelligence was meant to be used—creatively.

Right now I can hear a chorus of people wailing, "But I'm not creative!" Silence that chorus because it is a lie. Creativity is God's gift to us. Being and using our creativity is our gift back to God. Yes, you heard me correctly: you are creative. Let's stay with that thought and look more closely at verbal-linguistic intelligence. It's time to do some work.

A biblical encounter

As the catechists were coming through the door at a recent workshop, I stopped each one, gave him or her a slip of paper, and asked that they not tell anyone what was on the slip. Each one contained a name from the Bible: Eve, Moses, Mary Magdalene, John, Ezekiel, David, Ruth, and so on.

When everyone was seated, I told the group that they were to imagine themselves at a cocktail party. They were to get up and mill around, talking to one another. The only hitch was that they were to be the person on their slip of paper. If they had the name Moses, they were to answer questions and respond as they imagined Moses might. I emphasized that they were not to use their biblical names because I wanted the others in the room to guess as many of the "guests" as possible.

At my signal, everyone got up and began to talk to one another. Here's one conversation that I overhead:

"Hello, I can't believe all the work that needs to be done here."

"Work? What kind of work?"

"Where I come from people didn't have to work. That is until we didn't listen to the boss."

"I listen to the boss. In fact, I'm his favorite."

"His favorite? Does that mean you don't have to work?"

"No, silly. He just likes to tell me things, things to remember to tell others after he leaves us. In fact, I'm putting all this in a book so others can read about him."

"Hey," said a third person, "are you gonna put in those rules, I got from the big man?"

"I think those are already in an earlier book."

And so went the conversation between Eve, John the evangelist, and Moses. During the exercise the participants learned to look at biblical characters in a different way as well as find out what they did and didn't know about the person they represented. It was a great way to stretch the verbal-linguistic intelligence.

Now it's time for you to try your hand at creatively using your verbal-linguistic intelligence. Here are three phrases: *a sink; at a concert; in a fire.* With those three phrases, you are to make up a parable, one such as Jesus used. Imagine that you are teaching the people a lesson. What story will you tell them? Take time now to do this. Write down the story as it comes to you. Don't stop to correct spelling or grammar mistakes. Don't stop to think of the "right" thing that should happen. As you write ask the Spirit to guide you.

Here's what came from a workshop in Missouri (the participants had about five minutes to put this together):

> Once upon a time there was a sink. The sink was generally happy. Its job was to give a place for the water to run when people washed their hands or got a drink. The rhythm of the sink's life was unusual insofar as it lived in a concert hall and consequently went through times when it was very busy—during concerts, of course—and very bored—during the off-season.
>
> The sink, though, often felt that although it was doing what God wanted, it wasn't enough. Other people and things got to do great things, especially save lives. The sink never got a chance to do that—that is, of course, until the night of the big fire.
>
> Someone had left a candle burning and a strong draft had pushed the flame into the stage curtains which immediately caught fire. Because of the winter storm that was raging outside, the fire hydrant was of no help. The firemen looked desperately for something to use, beating at the flames with their coats in the meantime. Finally, one fireman happened on the sink. He took the faucet and attached the hose, turned on the water and directed it onto the flames. The water did its job and the theatre was saved.
>
> The sink, sooty and spent, smiled despite it all. Not only did it nourish people and keep them clean; in a real pinch, it helped save lives and property. As Christians, like the sink, we are called not only to do the ordinary but also at times, the extraordinary.

Now, this may not be a great literary effort, but everyone who experienced that story will no longer look at a sink in the same way. Each time they look at a sink, it will be a chance for an encounter with God and with their faith.

Whenever you see this sign, stop and do the exercise, or create a different exercise based on this one.

This exercise involves three cups. In one cup, place slips of paper carrying the name of an individual person or thing; for example: stopwatch, salesperson, boy, tiger, Indian, bee, teacher, television, mosquito, bear, anteater, dragon, bride.

In the second cup, place slips of paper on which you have written down the name of a place or an activity, such as at school, in a forest, in desert, at a funeral, jumping rope, trick-or-treating, at a mall at Christmas. For the third cup, write situations that would create a problem to be solved. These might include: having amnesia, discovering that a friend is missing, winning money, having an accident, being caught in a hurricane, losing a pet, being teased. Make the situations diverse enough, and cull them from the experiences of the people in your group or class.

When you are deciding what to put on the slips for the cups, be as creative as possible. Don't pass judgment on what you put on the slips of paper. When was the last time you saw an anteater in a parable? Just because you never saw one in a parable doesn't mean that an anteater in a parable isn't a good idea. Let your mind loose, and you will find that God speaks through many situations and many things.

Once you have put together the cups, have a person or group of persons pick one slip from each cup. Then instruct them to put together a parable just as you have done. You can allow them time to discuss what they will say, although I find this often stifles their creativity as they search for the right way to tell the story. Or you can simply have them come up with the story on the spot. Have the participants then share the parables with the larger group, then sit back and watch the connections to God take place.

Looking at faith in a new way

Sometimes we get into a rut when using verbal-linguistic intelligence, and only look at the surface knowledge. To move beyond this point, we have to consider our knowledge of faith in a new way.

Let's start by using the story of the prodigal son from the gospels. First of all, list all the people and things in the story. There are the two sons, the father, the pigs, the inheritance given to the son, the pigsty, the fatted calf, the party, and the hired hands. List everyone and everything you see as part of the story.

Now you or someone from the group will become one of the people or things listed; for example, someone will be one of the hired hands. Everyone else except the hired hand should then ask questions about the prodigal son, and the hired hand will answer to the best of his or her ability. It might go something like this:

"Could you tell us how you came to be in the employ of the father?"

"I needed work and I went everywhere searching. He hired me and I was certainly lucky. I can't think of anyone better to work for."

"What did you think of the two brothers?"

"Well, the one brother was very willing to help around the farm. He was pretty much a homebody. The younger one was kind of the restless type. He wanted to see the world. It was hard to keep him working on one thing. Many a time I had to follow up after him and fill in the holes. He wasn't always the most thorough worker. His brother was."

"What did you think when the younger son asked his father for his inheritance?"

"Frankly, I was shocked. It was almost as if he wanted the father dead so he could have his money. But, the more I thought about it, I think the son only saw it as a way to fill his adventurous spirit."

"How so?"

"He would be able to travel. See the world. Unfortunately, there are a lot of unscrupulous people out there, and they saw his money and lured him into doing things I don't think he really wanted to do."

"Like the gambling?"

"Yeah. That and getting involved with those women. He had never had a girlfriend before. And he hadn't had many friends because he wasn't away from the farm very often. When those unscrupulous cats said they liked him, he didn't want to lose their friendship. I think he gave them money whenever they asked. I don't think he spent it all on himself."

"What did you think when he came crawling back?"

"I think it took an awful lot of courage. Have you ever said you were wrong to someone? It's not the easiest thing in the world to do—and say it to your father to boot. I thought he had a lot of guts to come back, guts in the good sense."

"Were you surprised by the father's reaction?"

"Not in the least. As I said earlier, he is a very good man. I was lucky to be hired by him. He wants the best from everyone, and he forgives and forgets. It didn't surprise me that he would do the same for his son. His son was the important one. Nothing else."

"What did you think of the older son's reaction?"

"I think he forgot he had his father all the time. I think he just got a little jealous."

Now you try it. Let's say you are one of the threads on Jesus' robe. How would you answer some of the questions people would ask? What is a day with Jesus like? How did you feel when the woman who was bleeding touched the robe of Jesus and power went out of him? How does it feel to have no seams? What other encounters have you witnessed? What was it like knowing you became the possession of one of the Roman soldiers when they gambled for you? What was it like when you were ripped off of Jesus? How did the Roman soldier who won you react to you?

Those are just a few of the questions that might be posed to a thread from Jesus' robe. Add your own, then take time to answer all of the questions. You too will no longer be able to do simple sewing without thinking of Jesus. Your experience will shine in every stitch you take.

These activities help bring people with a dominant verbal-linguistic intelligence closer to God. The activities cause the mind to think more deeply and enable learners to experience and integrate the story into their being on different levels. Instead of the story being "out there," the story becomes part of the person and part of their faith life.

I often use parables to convey ideas because verbal-linguistic people enjoy stories as well as talking, writing, and reading. Jesus used a lot of parables. Although he did not refer to it this way, I think he had a great understanding of verbal-linguistic intelligence and the power it has to open minds and hearts. In the gospel of Matthew the apostles ask Jesus why he used parables.

> Then the disciples came and asked him, "Why do you speak to them in parables?"...[Jesus answered] "The reason I speak to them in parables is that 'seeing they do not perceive, and hearing they do not listen, nor do they understand.' With them indeed is fulfilled the prophecy of Isaiah that says: 'You will indeed listen, but never understand, and you will indeed look, but never perceive. For this people's hearts have grown dull, and their ears are hard of hearing, and they have shut their eyes; so that they might not look with their eyes, and listen with their ears, and understand with their heart and turn—and I would heal them.'" (Matthew 13:10, 13–15)

As Jesus advises, when teaching we must be careful not to close our ears and our own eyes, or the eyes and ears of those we encounter.

Maria Montessori, famed innovative educator, once said, "Education is acquired not by listening to words but by experiences." Words are an integral part of this intelligence, but it is not enough to just say them. We have to provide the experience. We take the words and bring them alive through the way we present them. And we can only do that if we are willing to risk and face our creative sides, to take a leap of faith into the unknown and trust that the Spirit will carry us to God.

There are several ways in which we take that leap of faith by using verbal-linguistic intelligence. The following are some activities that will get you started. Remember, though, as you read and perhaps use these ideas, that if you are committed to growth, you must use your own creative gifts to come up with other ways in which to reach people through their verbal-linguistic intelligence. If you only use what's here, your own creative side won't grow.

So I suggest that with these activities and those in subsequent chapters you try the idea. Then try the idea again with a change you've made. Next, try a totally different idea of your own. Keep the door open, and you'll be surprised at what comes in to greet you.

Remember, these ideas represent my own leaps of faith. Your responsibility is to take them beyond, to move forward on your own. It is helpful to keep a notebook handy and jot down ideas as they come to you.

○ *Now stop and do one or more of these exercises, or create one for yourself.*

REPORTING AS IT HAPPENS

Choose a Bible story or other well-known faith story and report it as if it is happening. Create a whole news program around a particular event. Involve as many people as possible and include interviews with individuals or things (such as the thread from Jesus' robe). Tell what the world looks like while the event is happening (maybe hearing from the fig tree), and don't forget to mention the weather.

THE GOSPEL ACCORDING TO ME

Have the children write a gospel. This gospel will tell others how they met Jesus, how they came to know Jesus better, and how Jesus is a part of their lives. Encourage them to include their own parables in their gospel and a timeline of events. The gospel can be illustrated, then bound into a small book by using a sewing machine.

LOOKING FROM THE BACK TO THE FRONT

Go over a familiar Bible story with your students. Make sure they know the Bible story very well. Now challenge them to tell the same story backwards. What new things are learned when the story is told this way?

WHO IS THE SECRET PERSON?

Pick a biblical or faith figure and take on their identity. A partner or the class has three minutes to interview you and guess who you are.

HOW ARE YOU?

Using the Bible, find as many different ways of greeting people as you can.

ONE WORD

Choose one word or name from the Bible and build a scene around it. Have the scene teach something about the life of Jesus or about our faith.

ONE WORD REVISITED

Choose a story from the Bible or a familiar faith story. Two people team up and, saying only one word at a time, they tell the story to the group. This is difficult but it teaches the importance of working together, building slowly, and becoming a community.

COMMERCIALS

Think of one thing about your faith you would like to sell. Prepare and present a commercial doing so. Videotape it if possible.

There. We have just listed eight ways of using verbal-linguistic intelligence in the classroom. Now, try to add eight of your own variations. Then see if you can come up with another eight completely original activities. Congratulations! You'll then have twenty-four exercises that appeal to verbal-linguistic intelligence for use in your religion classes.

Verbal-linguistic learners are sensitive to the sound, rhythm, and meaning of words. They are acutely aware of the different functions of language, and as a consequence are open to many teaching techniques, including poetry, humor, storytelling, grammar, metaphors, similes, abstract reasoning, symbolic thinking, conceptual patterning, reading, and writing.

Notice that reading and writing come at the end of this list of possibilities. Use the other possibilities first, and you will find that verbal-linguistic intelligence comes alive and guides you toward many powerful changes in your faith life and the faith lives of those you touch.

CHAPTER III

Logical-Mathematical

For just as the body is one and has many members, and all the members of the body, though many, are one body, so it is with Christ.

1 Corinthians 12:12

Math was never one of my strong points. In school I got by and even pulled A's in all my courses, but I still counted on my fingers in a pinch. You can imagine my amazement when someone once commented on my strong logical-mathematical intelligence. I thought they were crazy! What I failed to see at the time, however, and what I know now is that this intelligence is so much more than math problems. It is the intelligence that can quickly discern the existence of God.

Howard Gardner defines logical-mathematical intelligence as the sensitivity and capacity to spot logical or numerical patterns, and the ability to handle long chains of reasoning. Logical-mathematical children will be the ones in your religious education classes who know there were ten lepers and only one returned to give thanks. They will know the five loaves and two fishes story and its progression. They are conversant with the biblical numbers: twelve apostles, ten commandments, seven sacra-

27

ments, forty days in the desert. They know the importance of precision.

I once helped out at a high school youth retreat in El Paso, Texas. Several of the participants were from a small town called Marfa, which was in the middle of nowhere. Ghost towns sat on either side of it, and at night one could see the mysterious lights from the Chianti Mountains dancing. And it was Lando, a boy from Marfa, who showed me the power of faith.

The retreat director had brought along a jar of mustard seeds for his presentation on faith. "If we only have faith as big as a mustard seed," he said, paraphrasing Jesus, "we will be able to do anything." Lando was captivated by the size of the mustard seeds, each no larger than a speck of dust. After the presentation was done and everyone had left the meeting room, I came back to clean up. I found Lando still sitting at the table. The mustard seeds were laid out on a cloth and he was slowly, painstakingly counting them. Next to the pile of seeds was a paper filled with calculations.

"Lando, what are you doing?"

He looked up at me with a serious demeanor. "I'm figuring out a faith quotient."

"A faith quotient?"

"Yeah. I counted the number of mustard seeds. Each mustard seed represents one mustard tree. I took the average size of a mustard tree and then I multiplied that by the number of seeds in this jar." He looked at me with eyes wide. "Do you realize that if the people represented by this seed had the faith of a mustard seed, we would cover the earth with our faith? That's pretty amazing."

I was awestruck.

"Just think: if everyone had faith as big as a mustard seed, everything would be possible—and then some." He grinned at me. "Jesus had a pretty good idea. A little mustard seed goes a long way."

Jesus had a good idea, and Lando did too. His logical-mathematical mind brought home the possibilities of faith in a whole new way. Through his idea, I was able to see the meaning behind the parable of the mustard seed. Up to that point I had known what the story was about but had not really comprehended what it could mean. Lando made that a reality.

Reasoning toward God

Logical-mathematical intelligence is often linked with science. It is the scientific thinking that enables people to explore and see the progression of events through a given time period. The scientist's mind links up different factors and sees the relationship of one thing to another, arriving at a solution through steps following reasonably one after another. Because of this, a strong logical-mathematical intelligence can reason to the existence of God.

It was a beautiful spring day. I was teaching a preschool class at that time, and we were out on the lawn on our prayer blanket. The prayer blanket is a special blanket that we keep in the classroom and take out whenever anyone wants us all to pray to God in a special way.

This day, four-year-old Tracy asked to have the blanket taken out and said that she wanted everyone to pray about God. So there we lay, each child in his or her own place. Usually the children would close their eyes, but today Tracy instructed us to keep our eyes open as we prayed about God. I let my eyes wander across the turquoise blue sky, where large, fleecy cumulus clouds raced across the skyscape. A light breeze shook the tree limbs, heavy with spring buds. It was a beautiful day.'

I stole a look at the children. They too were taking in the sky, their eyes wide, their mouths solemn. From time to time one child or another would break into a smile. I settled back into my own thoughts, knowing that soon this time would draw to a close.

After fifteen minutes or so, I realized that it was time to wind up the lesson, go back inside, and get ready to go home. I started to sit up, and as I did, Tracy popped up along with each of the children in turn.

The children helped me fold the blanket and we headed inside. I had a funny feeling that our prayer had not been completed. But maybe our time outside wasn't meant to be prayer. Maybe it was just a nice day, perfect for watching the sky and the birds and the leaves.

Once inside I gathered the children in a circle to summarize our time together. Tracy tugged at my sleeve.

"Can I do this? We have to talk about our prayer." I looked down at her expectant face and nodded. The lesson could wait.

"So," she asked the others, "what did you learn about God during prayer?"

Michael's hand shot up. "If God created that big blue sky, then God must be very smart."

Libby's hand followed. "My dad makes clouds at work but they are never as big as God's. God must be lots smarter."

Billy wasn't going to be left out. "If you go back and back and back beyond the sky and beyond the planets and all the stars and things you have lots and lots of big stuff. But where did all that stuff first come from? It had to be God. Nobody here could've done it."

The conversation continued along these lines, affirming again and again the mightiness of God, the absolute existence of a power greater than that of people or nature.

Then it was Tracy's turn to speak. "When you were looking at the sky," she said to her classmates, "I was looking at the grass next to me. There was an ant and he was climbing on the grass. I thought, only God could make an ant that small and a blade of grass that fine, especially from a little seed." She looked at me. "That's why I wanted to pray about God. I think we all need to know God is here, especially when we forget or think God's not really real. God really is for real." Her big smile was the exclamation point to her statement of the reality of God.

The children arrived at their conclusions by using their logical-mathematical intelligence. Their reasoning went like this: if this was true about God, then that would be true about God. Hundreds of years ago, Heraclitus, a Greek philosopher, stated that the cosmos speaks in patterns and he urged the people of the day to look for the secrets of the universe in its patterns. What my preschool children were doing that day would have made Heraclitus proud. They were looking for *the* secret of the universe through the patterns around them. They were exercising their logical-mathematical intelligence well.

Going to trial

Putting logical-mathematical intelligence to use in the religion class was a challenge for me at first. I kept getting bogged down in the number aspect of this approach. It was only when I moved toward understanding the idea of logical patterns that I was able to see the potential for this intelligence in faith formation.

One of my first attempts at using this intelligence came when I was teaching social justice to a group of middle-schoolers. I spoke with them about the church's teaching in the area of social justice, and we talked about some real life situations. Yet too often during the session I would get the feeling that the students were giving me the answers they thought I wanted to hear. What I really wanted them to think about what was our responsibility as Christians in regard to social justice. I started to think my goal was impossible to reach when suddenly the Spirit intervened, and I was struck by an idea. We would hold a trial.

I decided to use the story of the woman caught in adultery. First, we discussed the law at the time of Jesus, which clearly stated that stoning was the punishment for such an act. Next, I chose children to represent the people involved in the situation—a judge, a prosecutor, a lawyer for the defendant, the woman, her mother and father, the townspeople, Jesus, his disciples, and a high priest from the temple. To add a different perspective to the story, I also asked one of the students to play the role of a mother whose daughter had been stoned the week earlier.

Time was given for the students to use Bibles and other reference books to prepare some ideas about their characters. The father thought about how he would feel about his daughter, the mother thought about life without her daughter, and the high priest, judge, and prosecutor all thought of the law. Each of the characters considered his or her motivation. Finally, it was time for the trial.

One by one the witnesses came forward and were questioned by the prosecutor and the defendant's lawyer. Since most middle school students are familiar with the police dramas of our time, it wasn't difficult for them ask questions of the witnesses:

"Would you tell us about your daughter?"

"She is a good woman. She is always willing to help around the house, ever since she was little. She must have had a reason for what she did. Please don't kill her."

"Would you state specifically what the law says?"

"A woman caught in the sexual act with another man who is not her husband is to be punished by stoning."

"And you, why did you have a stone in your hand?"

"I didn't have much to do today so I thought when I saw the crowd that it would be an opportunity for some excitement. Besides, I think the law says that people like her are supposed to be stoned to death."

"Why did you engage in such an act when you knew it could mean death?"

"My marriage has been a loveless one. My husband drinks all the time and refuses to even consider having children. Other than the day of our wedding, we have not made love to one another. This man offered me love and I was hungry for it."

"Jesus, what are your feelings on this?"

"She is basically a good woman. We all do things wrong. Who are we humans to judge another? Only God can judge. Only God knows what is in her heart."

And so it went. Finally the jury was cautioned by the judge to vote only on the information presented in the trial. The verdict was not guilty.

A lively discussion followed the trial, and led to talk about other social justice situations. With the use of their logical-mathematical intelligence, individuals are able to think out what they believe and why. No longer would they believe in something just because they were told to. They were now on their way to being people who know what they believe and have taken it to heart.

This is what God calls us to be—active thinkers. In the Book of Revelation, God urges us to take a stand, telling us of dire consequences. "Because you are lukewarm—neither hot nor cold—I am about to spit you out of my mouth"(Rev 3:15-17). Through logical-mathematical intelligence we can help ourselves and those we work with get in touch with what matters to them in their faith.

☺ *It's time now for you to try your hand at a logical-mathematical exercise.*

Use the format of the trial, as presented in the example above. Choose a story from the gospels or a current event. Determine what characters will be part of the trial. Look at the motivations of the accused. What aspects of the situation were not seen at first? What other scenarios might have occurred instead of what did occur? Have each character give a brief explanation about how their beliefs motivated their actions.

This activity can be used with many different age groups. It can reveal interesting dimensions to what we often see as black and white situations. It can help take our faith to a new level as we see God at work in different ways and in different settings.

The cost of poverty

Here is an activity that deals with hunger, and can be used with any age group. It has a strong logical-mathematical side where the participants experience the decision-making process as well as the consequences of their decisions. To begin with, divide the participants into groups of no more than six people each. These groups are considered families, and each family has 20,000 pesos for three days of meals. Each meal they purchase has to be enough to feed their entire family. The following is the shopping list available to them:

Chicken & red meat	9,000 pesos	1 meal
Fish	5,000 pesos	1 meal
Beans	2,000 pesos	5 meals
Eggs	1,000 pesos	1 meal
Potatoes	1,000 pesos	2 meals
Rice	500 pesos	5 meals
Carrots	1,000 pesos	4 meals
Squash	1,000 pesos	3 meals
Pineapple	1,500 pesos	1 meal
Apples	1,800 pesos	6 meals
Bananas	800 pesos	7 meals
Mangos	700 pesos	5 meals
Loaf of Bread	1,500 pesos	2 meals
Tortillas	1,000 pesos	8 meals
Bolillos (hard rolls)	1,000 pesos	5 meals
Powdered Milk	1,700 pesos	7 meals

Ask each family to draw a grid on a piece of paper similar to a tic-tac-toe board. The three columns across will be for breakfast, lunch, and dinner, while the three going down will be for Day 1, Day 2, and Day 3. Everyone can then start to figure out what they can afford for their meals, trying to keep the meals as balanced as possible.

After about five to seven minutes, inform the group that there is no clean water in the village and so each family must buy enough water for three days, for 2,000 pesos. Also remind them that they must pay 3,000 pesos rent for the land they live on. Let them begin balancing again.

After another five to seven minutes, interrupt the group to let them know that one of the children in their family has strep throat, and the medicine will cost 2,000 pesos. If they choose not to get the medicine, in all likelihood the child will die. If they do get the medicine, they must be careful there is still enough food to keep the rest of the family from getting sick.

Again, after five to seven minutes, interrupt to give the group the option of sending one of their children to school. The cost will be 8,000 pesos. Be sure to tell them that education is one of the primary ways for the family to move out of poverty.

In every group with whom I have conducted this exercise, be it grade school children or sophisticated adults, it has been an exercise in frustration. Above all, however, the participants are able to use their logical-mathematical intelligence to more clearly see the difficulties of the poor.

🕐 *Take some time now to consider how you might improve or change this exercise.*

Sometimes, multiple intelligence exercises are criticized as being "just play." In that case, I refer back to a book I read several years ago entitled *Godly Play*, by Jerome Berryman:

> Godly play is the playing of a game that can awaken us to new ways of seeing ourselves as human beings. It is the way to discover our deep identity as godly creatures, created in the image of God. The possibility of godly play puts the games played for glory, fame, and wealth, for "no aim," for home and family, for art or science, and even for salvation into a new and astounding frame...Godly play is a way to know God.

When we use exercises like the two above, activities that exercise our logical-mathematical intelligence, we are able to come to new realizations of who God is and what God calls us to be. These games enable us to approach our faith in a deeper, more integrated way.

Here are eight ideas for activities that use logical-mathematical intelligence. Remember, try these ideas, then try them with your own variations. Finally, try some totally different idea of your own. Your power of reasoning will strengthen, and your logical-mathematical intelligence will grow. *Don't forget to keep a notebook handy and jot down ideas as they come to you!*

To Tell the Truth

Choose three people to be Jesus or another faith character. As in the old TV game show of the same name, only one person will "tell the truth" in response to questions from the audience or from a chosen panel. Everyone then guesses who is the real person.

Time Lines

Pick a biblical event. Then, in three or four very short scenes, have a small group show the event unfolding across the period of a day or night. For example, if you chose Good Friday, you could act out a scene showing Jesus being beaten, one showing the struggle up to Calvary, and one with Mary weeping over her dead son.

Forensics

Choose a story from Scripture or a saint's life. Divide the group in two. One half will set the scene for the story. No people are in the scene, only clues that tell what took place. As an example, take the story in John 21:1–13, which tells of Jesus appearing to the apostles while they were fishing. Write out some clues to set the scene: drops of water, a dead campfire, a net, and a boat. Once the scene has been set, the other group tries to determine the story using only the clues given. Close the session by reading the story from Scripture or by the telling the saint's story.

Whose Future Is It?

One person is chosen to be a prophet, and he or she sits down, away from the group. Then, one by one, the prophet will then pick several familiar characters from the Bible or saints. (If you'd like, write up brief biographies ahead of time for the prophet to use.)

One by one, have people from the group sit down by the prophet and guess who they are by the clues about their future. For example: you will leave your wealthy home and to become a poor monk. You will travel throughout Italy and be known for your love of animals. You will be the founder of an order of priests that is still in existence today. (Answer: St. Francis of Assisi.)

NUMBERS

Using only numbers as your dialogue, carry on a serious conversation with a partner. What do the children learn during this conversation?

WHERE DO WE COME FROM?

String a clothesline across your classroom or meeting place. Have available a variety of materials—pictures, small objects of various kinds, artist materials, and so on. Make century markers, starting from 1 AD, on white posterboard beginning with creation or the birth of Jesus or another landmark event. then hang the posterboard on the clothesline.

Have participants list about twenty different events or people that they think are important and would like to know more about. Using the available materials have the participants create symbols for the events or symbols that represent the person's life. Have sourcebooks on hand to verify or look up information. Each player is then challenged to find out where on the timeline the event occurred or the person lived, and is instructed to pin the symbol to the appropriate place on the timeline.

After everyone has placed their objects on the timeline, talk about what they observed while they were doing this activity. What does this say about our Catholic faith and tradition?

INGREDIENT HUNT

Have the students look in Scripture in order to come up with the ingredients for this fruit cake.

3 cups of 1 Kings 4:22 (flour)

1 cup of Judges 5:25 (milk)

2 cups of Jeremiah 6:20 (sugar)

2 cups of Deuteronomy 23:25, dried and chopped (raisins)

2 cups of Mark 11:13, chopped (figs)

2 Tbs. of 1 Samuel 14:25 (honey)

2 tsp. of Genesis 19:26 (salt)

1/2 dozen of Job 39:14 (eggs)

1 cup of Genesis 24:30 (water)

2 tsp. of Mark 16:1 (spices)

2 tsp. of Galatians 5:9 (yeast)

Mix following Solomon's advice for making children good (Prov 23:14). Bake in a tube pan at 300 degrees for 2 hours. Test to see if the cake is done before removing from oven.

Any recipe can be adapted to these general ingredients. Other ingredients can be found during your own hunt through the Bible.

SEQUENCE STORY

Take a story from Scripture or from Christian tradition. Write out the story in your own words, then divide the story into sections. Mix up the sections, and give one section to each person. Keep aside the beginning section. When everyone has had an opportunity to read their section and reflect on it, tell the group that they are to determine where they come into the story.

Beginning with you, act out the first section, then ask the person who thinks they are next to come forward and act out their section. Then the next person comes forward and so on until all the sections have been read. Next, everyone tries to guess what the story is. If no one is able to, the process is repeated—but with a different sequence of readers. You will be surprised how mistakes in sequencing can affect the story.

Not only does this activity have great appeal for those with a strong logical-mathematical intelligence but it also appeals those who are predominantly verbal-linguistic.

So now you have eight ways of using logical-mathematical intelligence in your religion class. As before, try to add eight of your own variations, then see if you can come up with another eight completely original activities. If you maintain this approach in your teaching, you'll be surprised at the collection of activities you'll have by the end of the year.

Logical-mathematical people like to explore relationships and patterns. They like to experiment with things they don't understand, to ask questions, and to look into problems in a well-ordered way. They like working with numbers and enjoy solving problems. They learn best by looking for basic, common principles and patterns.

Regarding faith, logical-mathematical individuals learn best when they look to the traditions of our faith, our history, and the patterns of the universe. They relish the opportunity to reason through the existence of God. Remember the story of Clyde, the horse, from chapter one? Give the logical-mathematical children in your group the opportunity to explore their faith in logical and structured ways and, like Clyde, they will be challenged to go where they might not have gone before.

CHAPTER IV

Musical-Rhythmic

Make a joyful noise to the Lord, all the earth. Worship the Lord with glad-ness; come into his presence with singing.

Psalm 100:1–2

Adults were huddled in groups around tables. They were tapping, mak-ing noises with their mouths, slamming books against the table top, scratching their clothes, playing with their tongues, crumpling paper, and so on. Their assignment? To tell the story of the prodigal son using only sounds. No words were to be spoken. They were to use only the sounds in the room, either sounds they made or sounds already present, to tell the story.

After ten minutes of work, the room quieted down and the presenta-tions began. Those listening had their eyes closed. The story was being experienced in a unique and unexpected way. The anger, the happiness, the work, the sorrow, the elation at the son's return—each element of the story was communicated through sounds found in that room. It was a very powerful expression of musical intelligence.

When I first thought of musical intelligence, I assumed it meant the ability to sing or play an instrument. But I learned differently when I began to explore this intelligence in depth. Gardner defines musical intelligence as the ability to produce and appreciate rhythm, pitch, and timbre, and to appreciate various forms of musical expression. He also talked about this intelligence as being sensitive to the sounds of the environment and the human voice as well as to musical instruments.

The practical application of this intelligence came to me quite by accident. On this particular day, I was headed out to teach my preschool class. In the rush of trying to get out the door and to the church, I thought I had brought everything. When it came time to tell the Bible story for the day, however, I realized that my Bible storybook was missing. What could I do? I didn't want to tell the story in my own words since we had done that last time we met. Then it occurred to me: I would read the parable straight from the Bible. Perhaps I would have to change a few words, but that could be done and the children would get the gist of the story.

I began to read: "The kingdom of heaven is like the landowner of a vineyard who went out early in the morning to hire some people to work in his vineyard." My mind was racing. Should I change the word "vineyard"? What about "landowner"? I was so preoccupied with the "shoulds" and the "what ifs" that I finished the passage without changing any words. When I finished, one little hand shot up.

"Teacher, read it again." The freckle-faced youngster could barely contain his enthusiasm.

"Of course, Brandon, I'll read it again, but let's look at some of these words first."

"No, no," he interrupted. "Read it again just like it is."

And so I did. When I stopped and looked up, Brandon and two of the other children were swaying slowly. "What are you doing?" I tried to prepare myself for anything.

"It's the story," piped up Brandon. "It's like music when you read it."

Like music when you read it....

The concept of musical intelligence became clear to me that day through the simple words of Scripture. The Bible is a musical piece that touches the very heart of a person. God must have planned it that way. God's words touch human hearts in a way that is very basic, that reaches the depth of our person.

The silence of music

People with musical intelligence are attuned to the underlying musical current of life. They feel the rhythm of the world in their very being, along with the sounds of growth, the timbre of laughter, the pulse of work, the pitch of pain. They literally march to a different drummer, that is, the creative drummer of all life.

I saw this sensitivity nurtured in a Montessori classroom during an activity called the "silence game." The teacher begins the game by holding up a sign that reads "Silence." At this point all the children must try to be as quiet as possible. Not only do they keep from talking to one another, but they also close their eyes and try to keep their bodies motionless. They try to make no noise whatsoever in the classroom. After they have been quiet for some minutes, the teacher will generally whisper the names of the students one by one. When the child hears his name, he or she tiptoes very quietly over to the teacher's side.

Not only does this activity help the children learn to listen attentively, it makes them aware of the sounds in the classroom when all is quiet. They become attuned to the rhythm of the world around them and develop their musical intelligence in a very simple way.

This is not to discount those who sing or play an instrument. On the contrary, there are many expressions of musical intelligence. We have all had the experience of hearing a song that evokes a treasured memory or spiritual experience. Whenever I hear the song "Jesus Christ Is Risen Today," my mind is flooded with the memory of an Easter Sunday many years ago when I attended an early morning outdoor Mass of the

Resurrection. As the priest raised the host at the consecration, the sun rose and a flock of geese flew overhead. At that moment the enormity of Jesus' life, death, and resurrection filled my very being. When we sang "Jesus Christ Is Risen Today" at communion, I never felt more convinced or believed more in Jesus as savior than at that moment. Hearing that song today awakens all those memories once again.

Those who share their gifts through song or by playing an instrument are indeed doubly blessed with musical intelligence. Those who play or sing from the heart have a special ability to communicate the richness of God. It doesn't have to be a spiritual song in order for music to make us attuned to the higher mysteries. Many different kinds of songs can give us new meaning and insights into God. Too often we become schizophrenic as we try to separate the spiritual from the secular. But all things are spiritual for those who love God.

One song that unexpectedly draws me to God is a hit from the 1960s entitled "Wild Thing." While listening to this song some years ago, I heard the words for the first time: "Wild Thing, you make my heart sing./ You make everything groovy...." I thought about God singing this song to me, because I was God's wild creation. I did things that didn't always keep me going toward God, but God took pleasure in me nonetheless. No matter what I did, no matter if at times I chose poorly, God still loved me, loved me as God's own unique creation, as a special wild thing. Today I can never hear that song without remembering a God who loves me unconditionally and with a depth I shall never comprehend.

The Vatican II document on the Sacred Liturgy reads, "The Apostle exhorts the faithful assembled in expectation of their Lord's return to sing together, 'psalms, hymns and spiritual canticles' (Col 3:1). For 'singing is an expression of joy' (cf. Acts. 2:4). That is why St. Augustine rightly says 'it is natural for a lover to sing,' and an ancient proverb tells us 'the one who sings well prays twice.'"

"It is natural for a lover to sing." And yet in our liturgies we are often like people who are not in love. In a comedy sketch, British comedian

Eddie Izzard talks about singing in the church. He points out that in church, African Americans, a people who were enslaved and tortured and without a home for long years, take great joy in singing. On the other hand, Anglo Americans, people who have received much, who have power and money, and who lack very little, exhibit little joy in singing at church.

When we make use of the gift of musical intelligence, we are able to express the joy that comes from being in love with a God who cares deeply about us. It is important then, that we give our children opportunities to express that joy.

One of my most enjoyable experiences of musical intelligence took place in an adult education group where we were talking about story telling. After speaking about the various ways stories can be told, I challenged the group to come up with different ways to tell the parable of the sower and the seed (Lk 8:5–15). What came out of that session was a presentation I will treasure for the rest of my life.

Several members of the group got up and went to the front of the room. One of the people began to read from the Bible: "A sower went out to sow his seed…." Suddenly the group intoned these words, to the tune of "Tip Toe Through the Tulips":

Tip toe to the field, by the roadway,
That is where I'll be.
Come tip toe through the field with me.

The reading continued: "As he sowed, some fell on the path and was trampled on, and the birds of the air ate it up." One of the women cleared her throat, began to flap her arms and sang to the tune of "Up, Up, and Away":

Up, up and away with my beautiful bird seed….

A gentleman chuckled and continued the reading: "Some fell on the rock; and as it grew up, it withered for lack of moisture." With a little jaunty swagger, the group began to sing, to the tune of "Bye, Bye, Blackbird":

Pack up all your roots and go,
You're washed up,
You're dead, you know,
Bye, bye little seed.

They waited for the laughter to die down, then a young woman read: "Some fell among thorns, and the thorns grew with it and choked it." The audience heard the humming of the beginning of "Singing in the Rain," but these words followed:

I'm choking the plant, just choking the plant.
What a glorious feeling, I'm choking the plant.

Finally, we heard: "Some fell into good soil, and when it grew, it produced a hundredfold." With great enthusiasm, the chorus began to sing:

Everything's coming up roses for you and for me!

The presentation ended with a hearty proclamation, "This *is* the Word of the Lord." This presentation introduced me to a group of individuals in love with their God, not afraid to have fun with this and proclaim their feelings to the rooftops. Musical intelligence encouraged them to do so.

⊙ *Now it's your turn. Take one of the parables and make your own musical from it.*

Using our musical intelligence enables us to fall in love with God over and over again. It calls us to use the sounds of love to tell others how great is our God. When we open ourselves to our musical intelligence, we open ourselves to the Creator's music within us and our lives.

Here are eight exercises that use musical intelligence. Use them to begin to get in touch with the symphony that is God's kingdom.

SING A SCENE

Pick a Bible or faith story you know well. Decide who will play which part, then instruct the actors to sing their part. They can set the words to a melody of their own or to the tune of a popular song(s).

Rhythm Praise

Encourage people to begin with a prayerful intention of praising God. Have everyone sit in a row or in a circle. One person begins by clapping a pattern of four beats. The person next to him or her repeats the pattern and adds one beat. The next person does the same, and the next, each adding a beat. This continues until someone forgets the pattern.

Prayer Blanket

Choose a blanket that will be brought out only for prayer. Spread out the blanket and invite those who want to pray to join you on it. The only stipulations are that each person has his or her own space on the blanket, and that those on the blanket cannot touch one another.

People can either sit or lie down, whichever is more comfortable. Begin the prayer with a centering time, where all become quiet and close their eyes. Encourage everyone to pay attention to what is going on in their mind and outside of it. Tell them to listen to God speaking to them. After a period of time, ask everyone to open their eyes, sit up, and share what they heard.

The Blues

Ask everyone to think of something that makes them sad. Give them time to make up a song about this sadness—singing the blues, as it were. Give each person an opportunity to sing their sad song to God.

Paint a Song

Have art supplies on hand—paper, paint, crayons, markers, or whatever is readily available. Prepare some music to play, either spiritual songs, hymns, or other music. Direct the artists to paint what they hear God saying in the music. Are they inspired to use different colors? Different shapes? After each person is done, share the pictures and talk about what God said to them through the music, and how it made each person feel.

DANCING FINGERS

Ask everyone to bring in a pair of old gloves. Have on hand lots of buttons, needles, and thread (or glue if you are working with young children). Each person sews or glues a button onto each finger of the glove. After this is done, let everyone put on the gloves as you play a song—again, either a spiritual song or something else. Ask the people to move their fingers along with the music, as if dancing. Then talk about what God might be saying through this exercise.

THE DUELING DUET

Pick a familiar song and two people who will sing before the group. Have the two people sing together, trying to make it sound like they are one voice. This activity is an excellent way to bring home the idea of community prayer.

THE RHYTHM OF PRAYER

Have everyone gather in a circle around a table on which a group of candles has been arranged. Give each person a drum or some other rhythm instrument. As the candles are lit one by one, the people begin drumming or chanting. There are no rules about drumming; let it happen freely, from the heart. Ask the group to send thoughts of healing or peace to others, aloud. For example, "I send these thoughts to my brother that he may gain the gift of understanding." This is a variation on the prayer of petition. Bring the ceremony to a close when people finish sending out their thoughts. Let the drumming and the rhythm slowly die out.

As you use these exercises, remember to write down your own ideas. They can slip away as quickly as they came.

People endowed with strong musical intelligence include composers, musicians, performers, music teachers—and many people of deep faith. Music brings joy into life, whether through singing or playing instruments or through "life" sounds or other musical activities. As Thomas Aquinas said, "Joy is the human's noblest act." It is that joy which proclaims to the world our belief in a God who cares very deeply about us.

> Now to him who is able to keep you from falling, and to make you stand without blemish in the presence of his glory with rejoicing, to the only God our Savior, through Jesus Christ our Lord, be glory, majesty, power, and authority, before all time and now and forever. Amen. (Jude 24–25)

Feel the rhythm, the timbre, the pitch. Feel the joy in the God who made us. Feel your musical intelligence and praise God by using it yourself and with others.

CHAPTER V

Visual-Spatial

Then I saw a new heaven and a new earth; for the first heaven and the first earth had passed away, and the sea was no more. And I saw the holy city, the new Jerusalem, coming down out of heaven from God, prepared as a bride adorned for her husband.

Revelation 21:1–2

Remember the gospel story about Jesus talking to the apostle Thomas after his resurrection? Thomas had declared that unless he saw the wounds of his Savior, he would not believe. Jesus obliged and showed him, then said, "Have you believed because you have seen me? Blessed are those who have not seen and yet have come to believe." Thomas was a visual-spatial learner. He had to transfer what was in his mind's eye to something concrete, hence his need to see Jesus' wounds.

Visual-spatial people see a God that can't be seen by having concrete manifestations of that God. This is the intelligence of pictures and images. It is present in those people who can perceive the visual world accurately and then recreate their experience. They see form, color, shape, and texture in the mind's eye and are easily able to transfer those elements to concrete representations.

In the Science Center in St. Louis, Missouri, there is a hands-on exhibit where the participants are able to "operate" on a person. The only hitch is that the "doctor" has to look at a television screen in order to know where to place the instruments. The whole "operation" is done while looking at the screen. Some people come to this exhibit and leave very quickly when they find out how difficult it is to translate what they see on the screen to their hands. Other people—our visual-spatial people—can pick up the tools, watch the television screen, and effortlessly perform the surgery.

Another example is computer games, especially those that involve getting through mazes. For those not of a visual-spatial bend, it can be a frustrating exercise to cover the same territory again and again. Visual-spatial people have formed a picture in their head of the maze and are easily able to navigate through it. They are able to translate something flat to something dimensional. These are the same people who can come into a room, look at it and quickly determine what colors would go well in the room. In our churches these are the individuals who are able to decorate the church in such a way that the spirit of a particular season becomes palpable.

One of my first experiences of visual-spatial intelligence in the religious education classroom came during a session with fifth graders on reconciliation. To illustrate themes of forgiveness, we used a play about a town called Vengefulville. In this town each person wore a badge around their neck. When they ran into another person, if that person perceived he or she had been hurt by the other, he or she would pull out a hole punch and put a hole in the other person's badge. Seven holes in your card meant that you would be put to death.

People would often be "hole punched" because of a simple accident. "Oops, I'm sorry" didn't mean anything to the people of Vengefulville. A hurt was a hurt and that meant a punch for their card. There was no forgiveness. As a consequence, very few people were out on the streets. Stories were told of various residents who had six punches and now didn't even go out of their houses for food.

Because of the hole punch practice, the population of Vengefulville grew smaller and smaller. When a stranger came to town and talked about forgiveness, his card was soon filled up with punches. It was not a happy place. The play ended on that note.

As we sat talking about the play, one boy raised his hand.

"I'm glad God doesn't keep score like this."

"Want to say more, Randy?" I could assume what he meant but I wanted to be sure.

"If God punched our cards like they did in Vengefulville, we'd only last an hour, maybe two. Lots of what we do to hurt people comes out of thoughtlessness, and in Vengefulville this is a crime punishable by death." He looked around the room at the actors who had their badges hanging around their necks, the holes attesting to the fact that very few of them would be with us very long.

Then Randy picked up a circle from the floor and walked over to one of the actors. "Here," he said, placing the circle back in a hole. "This is what Christians are supposed to be about. Filling the holes."

By using his visual-spatial intelligence, Randy was able to see the concept of forgiveness in a very concrete way. Christians are the people who would refuse to punch another's card, who would fill the hole with one from their card. Christians are people of forgiveness. They could change Vengefulville.

The story of Vengefulville is an excellent source of wisdom for the visual-spatial child. Not only can he or she see forgiveness being played out, but he or she can see the damage done by sin, thoughtlessness, and insensitivity.

Imaging God

On another occasion, I was observing a confirmation class of high school students who were discussing their images of God. After a while, the teens were divided into groups, and each group was challenged to come up with an image of God. Several of the groups just polled each other on concepts of God that were important to them, then created an image of God that incorporated these concepts.

One group, however—which I suspect was heavily visual-spatial—decided to portray their image on a banner. I didn't see any conversation after the project was begun, and each person seemed to be working on their own section of the banner. Clearly this would not be a composite image of God.

How wrong I was. As the exercise was winding down, the group created a giant bottle of Elmer's glue which they pasted on one corner of the banner. They then drizzled glue and laid string from one section of the banner to another, and wrote out a slogan at the top "God, the Glue Used by Different People in Different Ways." For this group, each individual image of God needed to remain separate; yet each image needed to be interwoven into one. This group used their visual-spatial intelligence to communicate this message in very concrete terms.

One of the best ways I have found to nurture visual-spatial intelligence is the object exercise. Many people have had the experience where they buy a car, and suddenly it seems as if every third person has this very same car. Or when a woman is pregnant, suddenly she seems to run into pregnant woman after pregnant woman. This is what is known as a mindset. When our minds are absorbed or directed in a particular way, we become acutely aware of the things around us that fit into that way of thinking.

When you create a mindset of God, you become acutely aware of how things around you connect to God.

Begin this activity with peanut butter. I challenge you now to take a few minutes and write down at least ten ways in which peanut butter is like or connects to God.

My list reads: God is like peanut butter because, like peanut butter, God sticks with you. Peanut butter is a staple in most homes, and God should be a staple in your life. Peanut butter is nutritious, containing protein and lots of vitamins to help people grow. God is very healthy for our lives and helps us grow. Choosy moms choose peanut butter, and choosy people choose God. And we could go on....

Now try the word "book." Mine might read: God is like a book because God is full of knowledge. God is like a book because God takes us to places we have never seen before. There are many sides to God as there are many books in the library or bookstore. Books help when we need them, just as God is there to help us when we need God. And so on.

The object exercise helps visual-spatial intelligence people bring their images of God into concrete terms. Using this exercise can help anyone better develop his or her visual-spatial intelligence, and create a mindset that connects everyday objects to God. Everything around us comes from a divine source. When we become aware of this we begin to move closer to God, who then begins to permeate our lives.

Some of the first words both of my children learned were "come and see." Whenever a new discovery was made, whenever something happened, the words "come and see" invited, cajoled, and kept me running time and again throughout the day. Sometimes it was a bug or a flower, or the ability to do little things for themselves. All these were moments of God for my children. And all these moments helped me become ever more aware of the fact that God permeated my life and the lives of those around me. God wasn't hiding. God was right there in front of our faces, time and time again. If I wasn't aware of that, it was often because I had failed to look, to become aware, to act with my visual-spatial intelligence.

Let's look at other ways you can nurture visual-spatial intelligence in your classroom. Remember, visual-spatial people like to be both concrete and abstract at the same time.

MARKING TIME

When you introduce a topic for a new lesson or unit, draw an hourglass on the blackboard or on a piece of posterboard. Talk about how this exercise will help us see what we know and what we wonder about. Have the children brainstorm about everything they already know about the topic. Write the items on the upper portion of the hourglass. Then brainstorm all the questions the group has about the topic, including "what if" questions. Write these in the lower portion. You can then ask different individuals to take a question and research the answer. Later, they can present their findings to the rest of the class.

REBUS

A rebus is defined as a representation of words in the form of pictures or symbols, often presented as a puzzle.

Show a sample of a sentence using a rebus. Brainstorm some ideas from a particular lesson you are working on. Have the children make up sentences by using a rebus of one or more of the concepts they have learned. They can work in small groups if so desired. When everyone is done, share the rebuses with the group, and have the rest of the group guess the sentence.

MYSTERY TRAY

Choose a special tray that will be designated as the mystery tray. On the tray place an object connected with the concept being studied, but don't let anyone see the object ahead of time. Cover the object and place it in view of the participants. Ask them to guess what might be on the tray. They can ask questions about the object, to which you answer only yes or no. This exercise forces the group to make connections between the abstract and the concrete.

CARTOON TIME

Choose a cartoon strip and white out the dialogue in the bubbles. Talk to the group about particular concepts you are studying. Have each child choose a concept and then write new dialogue for the blank bubbles to express these ideas. They can also incorporate their personal thoughts and feelings about the concept into the cartoon strips.

TREASURE BOX

Give each child a box with a lid, such as a shoe box, and ask them to decorate the box (this can be done at home, if more convenient). Explain to them that they will be putting symbols of what they are learning into the box. Some of the symbols will be supplied by you, while some of them will be created by the children themselves. These are to remind the students what God is teaching us.

BUILDING THE CHURCH

Supply plenty of Lego blocks or other building materials. Have the participants design a church, either individually or in groups. What is an outward symbol of their inward symbol of church?

MAPMAKER, MAKE ME A MAP

Make a map of what you are studying. For example, you can map out the field where the sower works, or the route to Calvary. Map out the city of Bethlehem or the Upper Room where the Last Supper took place. Be sure and place all the important places on this map.

A FAITH MACHINE

Divide the class into groups and have them design faith machines. What would this faith machine do? What would you put into it? What would it dispense?

Visual-spatial intelligence people can form pictures in their minds. In a sense, they can see the unseen. Like the apostle Thomas, they find it easier to make a leap of faith when they are able to make a connection between the picture in their mind and the concrete. These people are our navigators, our sculptors, our architects, our painters, and our graphic design artists. They are the people who add dimension to our lives—and the people who, when invited, can add dimension to our faith.

CHAPTER VI

Bodily-Kinesthetic

Run in such a way that you may win the prize. Athletes exercise self-control in all things; they do it to receive a perishable garland, but we an imperishable one.

1 Corinthians 9:24–25

You can't breathe very well if your heart isn't beating or your blood isn't circulating. So too, you can't grow in faith if your joy isn't nurtured or your anger isn't expressed. We need to address the whole of our beings, and bodily-kinesthetic intelligence helps us do that.

We needn't be afraid of expressing ourselves with our bodies. We needn't worry that our actions will be sacrilegious. Rather we need to be concerned that if we emphasize bodily-kinesthetic intelligence in our faith practices, we will have to energize our worship, our education, and our parish interactions. Too many of us have been dulled by inactivity, to a rather static approach to faith—at least in the area of bodily expression. Here I challenge you to change that.

Howard Gardner defines bodily kinesthetic intelligence as the ability to use the body to express emotion, as in dance, body language, and sports. He says that it is the ability to learn by doing. It is the intelligence of the whole body. You can't be bodily-kinesthetic and not move.

Babies and toddlers provide a good example of bodily-kinesthetic intelligence. All their experiences come in through the body. They are constantly touching, holding, moving, or dancing. Everything they encounter comes under close scrutiny by their bodies and is manipulated by their hands. As adults, we're not used to putting our bodies to such extensive use—witness the exhausted parent who tries to keep up with a toddler! Most of us would much rather sit and talk. We have gotten out of touch with our physical selves.

Bodily-kinesthetic intelligence motivates us to interact with the world around us and process the knowledge we receive through bodily sensations. In the late 1960s and early '70s, there was a move in religious education toward sensory exercises that emphasized the tactile nature of God; for example: take an apple. Hold the apple. Smell the apple. Look closely at the apple. Taste the apple. In short, get to know this apple. Exercises such as this involved the physical senses. Looking back, I would guess that much of the embarrassment people felt with these tactile experiences came from being out of touch with their bodily-kinesthetic intelligence.

Bodily-kinesthetic intelligence can be easily spotted in people. They are the ones who have difficulty sitting still or staying in their seats for long periods of time. They make generous use of body gestures to express themselves. In a classroom, they are often the first offering to demonstrate to others how to do something.

One of the practices I adopted early on with all of my classes, children and adults alike, was a modified form of yoga. I had come across a variation called "animal yoga" in a great science book by Susan V. Bosak, *Science Is...*. We would usually begin with a pose called Fly Like a Bird. To start, the participants put their arms at their sides, lean forward, and then slowly lift their arms behind their back. Hold this position for a count of five, then relax. There were other positions that we used; for example, the Jellyfish, Yawn Like a Lion, and Kneel Like a Camel. My classes usually enjoyed the exercise and had a good laugh at the same time.

My practice of animal yoga was expanded with a group of forty tenth graders who were gathered together for a confirmation program. We were focusing on the qualities of decision, commitment, and witness critical to this sacrament, and had come to a break in the program. I decided to introduce the teens to animal yoga as a way of stretching and relaxing. We were just into the fourth animal when one of the tenth graders piped up: "Why don't we do confirmation yoga?"

"Confirmation yoga?" I was puzzled.

"Okay," she said. "Let me teach you." Laura came to the front of the room, nodded at me, and began. "This is Rodin's Decision. First you put one foot slightly in front of the other. Crouch a bit. One arm is by your side, the other comes up and cups your chin. You squint your face like this." I watched as she assumed the pose of Rodin's famous sculpture, the Thinker.

Laura encouraged everyone to take this pose, and soon we had a roomful of decision-making people. Following in quick succession were poses for commitment and for witness. For the rest of the session, these poses became second nature. The teens would lapse into them during a presentation or while waiting for a snack. Though lighthearted and fun, this exercise nevertheless reinforced the themes of decision, commitment, and witness through the use of bodily-kinesthetic intelligence.

Following Jesus

Perhaps you've seen the episode of *I Love Lucy* where Lucille Ball meets Harpo Marx and in one of the scenes, she mirrors his moves. I tried this once with a group of drama students. As we were going through the exercise, the Spirit spoke, and I realized that mirroring would be an excellent way to teach the importance of following Jesus. I decided to try it at my next religious education gathering, which turned out to be a with a group of middle school students.

As the Spirit would have it, we were studying the call of the apostles. I had the children line up in two rows and stand opposite each other. Then I asked them to think of what they do in the morning in front of the mirror. Do they brush their teeth? Do they put on makeup? Do they comb their hair? After they had some time to think about these activities, I chose one side to be the "doers" and the other to be the "mirrors."

When I told them to begin, the mirror person tried to follow the motions of the doer opposite him or her. Needless to say there was bedlam and giggles and "aw, gees," but this exercise did get across the point of how difficult it is to follow someone. We repeated the activity several times through the year, always discussing what it means to follow, how we follow, and what makes it so difficult.

I like to incorporate bodily-kinesthetic intelligence into my lessons on the Eucharist by having the children make their own altar bread. I start by making the flour with them. The first step in preparing the flour is to grind it from wheat, and we use a mortar and pestle for this step. It's a challenge to learn how fine the flour must be before it can be used for making bread, but I can always count on my bodily-kinesthetic intelligence people to demonstrate how fine it should be. After one explanation during the year, I generally do not have to explain it again. The children who are strong in this intelligence do this for me.

I'm in love with bodily-kinesthetic intelligence because it speaks to me of the art forms that strongly emphasize the beauty of creation. Have you ever watched an ice skating exhibition and not been moved by the fluidity of the motion? Have you ever marveled at the strength of the swimmer as he or she cuts through the water with the difficult butterfly stroke? Have you been astounded by the pure poetry in motion of seeing a juggler perform a complicated routine?

Jesus was probably in touch with bodily-kinesthetic intelligence because Joseph, his father, was a carpenter. I picture Jesus sitting in Joseph's shop, watching intently as his father whittled and created things, observing Joseph as he prepared the wood, and trying his own hand at bringing a creation out of a piece of wood.

God speaks of bodily-kinesthetic intelligence when we hear about the potter in the Book of Jeremiah:

> The word that came to Jeremiah from the Lord: "Come, go down to the potter's house, and there I will let you hear my words." So I went down to the potter's house, and there he was working at his wheel. The vessel he was making of clay was spoiled in the potter's hand, and he reworked it into another vessel, as seemed good to him. Then the word of the Lord came to me: Can I not do with you, O house of Israel, just as this potter has done? says the Lord. Just like the clay in the potter's hand, so are you in my hand, O house of Israel. (Jeremiah 18:1–6)

A hands-on God

Our God is a very hands-on God. After all, a God who gives us flowers and oceans and birds and people and all sorts of interesting things—and who didn't put a "Do Not Touch" sign on any of these things—is a God who wants us to become intimately involved with creation. This means being hands-on as we learn about God both for ourselves and for the children and adults we work with.

An activity that is a favorite among children in preschool religious education is the fishing lake. A small lake is cut out of blue plastic then filled with fish, cut out of colored paper with a paper clip glued on the nose. The boat is made from a large cardboard box, large enough for two children; for the fishing pole, tie a string to a sturdy piece of doweling and attach a magnet to the end of the string.

The children climb into the boat to fish. Using hand-eye coordination they work diligently at catching all the fish. When fishing is done, the children tell the rest of the class what they learned about God during their fishing trip. One time I was graced with the comment from a four-year-old girl who stated, "Some of those fish keep trying to get away. I guess that's like the people who keep trying to get away from God."

One of the greatest gifts that came out of Vatican II was the revival of liturgical dance. Not only were we able to see dance as part of our worship, we began to see dance as a way to express our faith.

In the religious education classroom, dance can offer children a chance to actually feel their faith. One of the dances that I do with third graders is the story of Noah's ark. First we read the story as it is told in Genesis. Then we talk about the important elements of the story, starting with the building of the ark. Here the children act out the process, hammering, sawing, fitting the pieces together, and painting. Noah and his family move into the ark, followed by different animals (you can be sure the children have a wonderful time imitating elephants with swinging trunks, long-necked giraffes, and lumbering lions!)

Interest picks up as the storm begins, and we consider how to express the storm with dance. Wildly falling rain, loud claps of thunder, and swirling waters come alive in one flowing movement. By the time we are finished we have brought the story of Noah to life through dance. The children's whole bodies have felt the story, and they have integrated it into their hearts.

Take a few minutes now to consider how you could use dance in your teaching. Try to be as creative as you can. Remember that since we ourselves are creations of God, we are meant to continue the process by being creative ourselves.

Here are some jumping off exercises to incorporate bodily-kinesthetic intelligence into your teaching. Remember to take the exercises one step further and to create one of your own, if you can, for every one listed here.

SHOES OF JESUS

Have everyone sit in a circle, remove their shoes, and place them in the middle of the circle. Talk about the features the shoes have in common and those that make the shoes unique. Next have each person take a pair of shoes not their own and attempt to put them on. One thing they will discover is that it's difficult to walk in someone else's shoes. What other insights surface from this activity?

WHO AM I?

This is a game of charades with a time limit. Put the names of various people of faith into a hat. One person picks a name and uses his or her voice and body to become that person, but they cannot say who they are. Give the actors three minutes before they reveal their identity.

PUPPET PERSON

Choose a story from the Bible or from Catholic history. One person tells the story to the group while the other acts out the story as it is being told.

GOD DANCE

(This is an individual activity that can be adapted for a class.) Make up a dance to communicate something you are feeling—the greatness of God, sorrow at a loss, the need for help, gratefulness for something in creation. Decide on the music you will use and what you will wear. Practice the dance, then perform it for others or in quiet before God.

PRAYER DRAMATICS

Take a prayer that is familiar and ask people to act out the prayer in different ways: as if they are describing a mystery; really bored; reading a recipe; very nervous; terrified; elated; and so on. Talk about how prayer covers all our emotions and how we must guard against our prayer becoming routine, that is, words without feeling.

CLOSING THE SALE

Select one person to be the salesperson, and the rest of the group will be the clients. Plan a way to sell your faith to them. Remember to be honest about your beliefs. Use humor, pathos, and care in your presentation.

Rituals Alive

Have the group decide on a particular event they would like to mark with a ritual. Let them brainstorm ways in which to do it. Set a time limit for the ritual. You might even suggest they address the multiple intelligence during the ritual so it can appeal to everyone. Set aside a special time to have the ritual and celebrate the event.

Fruit Basket Mix-up

Originally this game was done with fruit names, hence the title. I have found that it can be applied to many faith formation situations with great results. Suppose you are studying reconciliation. Think of key words regarding reconciliation: sin, sorrow, forgiveness, confession, and penance. Set up a circle of chairs with one less than the number of participants. Give each person a word (some people will have the same word), and have one person stand in the middle of the circle. He or she can choose to say one of the key words or simply the word "reconciliation." When a person's word is spoken, he or she must get up and find a new chair. When "reconciliation" is said, everyone must get up and find a new chair. The person left standing in the middle calls the next word or "reconciliation."

To insure safety, set out some rules at the start of the game. Anyone who is sitting next to an empty chair is to hold it steady for the person who might come to sit in it. Also, although this game takes a lot of movement and can be rowdy, caution them that the game will end when a chair goes over—this is usually an indication that the game is getting too rough. This game can be used with many different topics, for example the ten plagues, Lent, the twelve apostles, and so on. Use your imagination.

Finding our treasure

In his book, *The Treasure*, Uri Shulevitz tells about a man named Isaac who lived in great poverty and who often went to bed hungry. One night

Isaac had a dream in which he was told to go to the capital city and look for a treasure under the bridge by the royal palace. Of course, Isaac paid no attention at first but when the dream was repeated night after night, he decided to make the journey.

It was a long journey through forests and up mountains. Sometimes people gave him a ride, but most of the time he walked. When Isaac finally arrived at the capital city, he went to the bridge by the royal palace. There he discovered that the bridge was guarded day and night, and so he couldn't search for the treasure. Nevertheless, each day he went to the bridge and wandered around it until dark.

One day, the captain of the guards asked Isaac why he was there. When Isaac told him, the captain laughed and said, "You poor fellow! What a pity you wore out your shoes for a dream. Listen! If I believed a dream I once had, I would go right now to the city you came from, and I'd look for a treasure under the stove in the house of a fellow named Isaac."

Upon hearing this, Isaac returned to his home and dug under the stove. There he found the treasure! In thanks he built a house of prayer, and in the corner he put the inscription, "Sometimes one must travel far to discover what is near."

We are so like Isaac as we go in search of our treasure. We go to seminars. We search out speakers on various subjects. We try different prayer paths. We desperately try to find a way to ease ourselves out of our poverty of spirit when the opportunity to do so is right in front of us.

Bodily-kinesthetic intelligence—if we work to awaken it, to strengthen it, and to celebrate it—helps to erase our poverty of spirit. The tools are always right with us, much like Isaac's treasure. One tool is our body, the treasure that can take us and those we minister with to a deeper understanding of God's love for us all.

CHAPTER VII

Naturalist

*From the fig tree learn its lesson: as soon as its branch becomes tender and
puts forth its leaves, you know that summer is near. So also, when you see
all these things, you know that he is near, at the very gates.*

Matthew 24:32–33

My mother always had us work in the garden on Good Friday. It was
important, she said, to get in touch with the soil on this day. So as we
weeded and dug and planted, she would tell the seven of us children how
moist, dark soil is placed on bodies when they are buried and how,
because of Jesus, this isn't the end. There is new life that comes from the
earth, like the flowers or the weeds. I don't think my mother realized it,
but she was giving us a taste of what it is to use our naturalist intelligence.

Gardner defines naturalist intelligence as the ability to discriminate
among living things, as well as sensitivity to other features of the natural
world. Most individuals graced with a strong naturalist intelligence have
a keen ability to recognize and categorize plants, animals, and other
objects in nature. Thomas Armstrong, a strong proponent of multiple
intelligence, further sees this intelligence as the capacity to see nature

operating on a larger scale. How does nature interact with civilization? What are the symbiotic relationships in nature? How do life cycles impact us?

Pope John XXIII was someone with a strong naturalist intelligence. This came through in his encyclical *Peace on Earth*, where he wrote about the importance of order in both the universe and in human beings:

> Peace on earth, which people of every era have most eagerly yearned for, can be firmly established only if the order laid down by God be dutifully observed. The progress of learning and the inventions of technology clearly show that, both in living things and in the forces of nature, an astonishing order reigns, and they also bear witness to the greatness of people, who can understand that order and create suitable instruments to harness those forces of nature and use them to humanity's benefit.

The pope goes on to address the concept of order in different realms of life, and how important this is to achieving peace. This quality of order is very important to the naturalist intelligence.

The first time I learned about the importance of this great truth was in a Montessori classroom. I knew very little about Montessori at that time, and I did not have a very good concept of the theory of education behind this method of teaching.

My son Nathaniel, who was then three, had been in this particular school for about two weeks. He had come in to the classroom looking for his favorite activity, but after about five minutes of searching the room, he went up to his teacher. "Pat, I can't find the farm. Where is the farm?"

"I had to put it away, Nathaniel. There were pieces missing and so you couldn't build the whole barn. We'll wait to put it out until all the pieces are present." The teacher wasn't being mean, and she wasn't angry because the children had misplaced some of the pieces. Instead, she was being very attuned to order, which is one of the components of Montessori education.

There is purposeful activity in the Montessori classroom. The room itself reflects the structure and order of the universe as God made it. Here the child learns to trust the environment and his or her power to interact with it in a positive way. The child is assured of a completed cycle in the process of learning play: all the pieces of an activity are there when the child picks it up; there is no interruption when he or she is doing an activity; and the materials are returned, complete, to the same place each time. The naturalist intelligence thrives on order, and Nathaniel was learning this from his experience with the missing pieces of the farm.

An ordered faith life

Structure and order are not only important to our daily life but to our faith life as well. Religious practice is full of order and ritual. There is a structure and order to our worship, to our movement in faith. When this is present in the classroom, it moves a child to realizing the sense of order implicit in the universe, the organizing power of the presence of God. In the beginning of the Book of Genesis, we read how "the earth was a formless void," and God stepped in to bring order to this chaos.

People with naturalist intelligence make distinctions in the natural world. To them, beans are not just beans. What kind of beans are they? Pinto, kidney, or black beans? They are not just seeds. They are marigold, bachelor button, or zinnia seeds. So how does all of this relate to faith formation? Let's start with Psalm 95, verses 8–10:

Do not harden your hearts, as at Meribah,
as on the day at Massah in the wilderness,
when your ancestors tested me, and put me to the proof,
though they had seen my work.
For forty years I loathed that generation and said,
"They are a people whose hearts go astray,
and they do not regard my ways."

This psalm tells of the people of Israel who were turning a deaf ear to

God; they were hardening their hearts. How can a soft heart become hard as a rock? My class of sixth-graders was going to find out.

We would test this by seeing how soil could be soft in some places yet hard in others. To begin, we armed ourselves with four cans from which the top and bottom had been removed, then trooped out into the yard that was connected to the church. We put the cans in various places in the yard—the walkway between the church and the hall, the garden full of flowers, an area close to the fence, and the newly tilled soil in a corner of the yard. I then gave the students four sticks that had been cut from doweling to twelve-inch lengths, and they went around the yard trying to push the sticks into the ground in the middle of the cans.

"Wow! Look at that! It's only got a couple of inches showing." The stick went easily into the soil of the tilled garden.

"This one goes in pretty far. There's about half of the stick showing." A daffodil looked on in interest as another stick went into the garden soil. Over by the fence, the group had a bit of trouble getting the stick in. "It goes in but not very far. There must be about nine or ten inches showing. Let's measure." So the measuring tape was brought out and each stick was measured: one inch showing in the newly tilled soil; five and a half inches in the flowers; eight and a quarter inches over by the fence.

"Wait, we forgot the walkway." All of us walked over to see how far the stick would go in here. We gently pushed the stick into the top of the soil, but it wouldn't budge. We tried another time, but nothing. Finally, on the third try, it looked as if the stick might break so we stopped. "We can't even get this one in."

I looked at the students and said, "What do you think this has to do with the Israelites who were turning a deaf ear to God?"

They turned and looked at the cans. One pig-tailed girl piped up. "The people were hearing God in various ways. Some were really ready— like the soil where the stick went right in—and some were sort of ready. But," she said turning to the empty can, "some were so deaf God couldn't even start to get in."

In that moment, the wonder of our faith was spoken through the dirt. God's message had come home in a very real and ordered way. Now give yourself a chance to see how you can use the natural world to bring home a faith principle.

⏱ *You can do an interesting variation of the above activity by centering it around the parable of the sower and the seed.*

Read the parable to the class, then ask each child to bring in three samples of soil, each sample from a different place. When you have all the samples together, tell the children you are going to look at the soil samples together and determine in which soil the seeds would grow very well, sort of well, not so well, and not at all. After this discussion, ask the group to describe the types of people represented by their soil samples.

If you wish, you can take this activity a step further and have them write their own version of the parable of the sower and the seed.

It doesn't take a great deal of effort to awaken the naturalist intelligence. After all, nature is all around us and we can easily make good use of it. I found a great science exercise in the *Science Is...* book, mentioned in an earlier chapter, and I was able to adapt it for my faith formation sessions.

Begin with an empty plate, which represents the bedrock of a river. Talk about how the river flows over the igneous bedrock. As the years go by, sand is pressed down by the water and cemented together to form white sandstone. (Now put a slice of white bread on the plate.) Talk about how one year, there was a major flood. Tons of mud and rocks swept over the sandstone. (At this point spread chunky peanut butter on the bread to represent the mud and rocks. You might also add some raisins for boulders.) The river keeps flowing, and now the water carries small bits of rock called silt. Over many years this silt turns to shale. (Use a slice of brown bread to represent the shale.)

By now we have reached the end of the Ice Age and the glaciers are melting. The oceans rise and cover everything. Creatures in the water die over time, and their shells and skeletons become part of the ocean floor.

After many years these become limestone. (At this point, spread a thick layer of jam on the brown bread.) Now there is a bad drought with strong winds picking up particles of eroded rock. The particles blow against the mountainside, and a layer of brown sand forms. (Finish the sandwich with a slice of dark rye bread representing the brown sandstone.) You now have a great sandwich for showing how rock layers were formed—but also for showing the many aspects of faith development.

The plate is Jesus, the bedrock, who holds us up. The white bread is the purity of our souls as we start out life. The peanut butter and raisins are the different aspects of life that cause us either to grow or to draw away from Jesus. The brown bread symbolizes our growth in faith, integrating the different aspects in our life, both good and bad. The jam points to the peak experiences that are part of faith growth, and the dark rye bread speaks to the integrated Christian. Take the sandwich and bend it to show how all these aspects are integrated together. None stands alone; all point to growth.

What could this sandwich exercise represent to you in regard to faith? Perhaps you can vary the ingredients to suit your own ideas.

Challenges for the naturalist intelligence

Scripture gives us plenty of opportunities to challenge the naturalist intelligence. On Palm Sunday, we hear these words from the gospel of John: "They took branches of palm trees and went out to meet him, shouting, Hosanna! Blessed is the one who comes in the name of the Lord—the King of Israel!" (12:13) Have the class research the type of palm that was native to the Holy Land. What did it look like? Is it like the palms we receive today on Palm Sunday? What does it symbolize?

Or take another lenten gospel story, that of Jesus' temptations in the desert (Mt 4:1–11). Not all deserts are alike. What kind of hardships might Jesus have faced in the deserts of the Holy Land? What types of animals would he encounter? Take this exercise further, and look at the story of the Israelites as they wandered through the desert (Ex 16—17). What dangers faced them during their time in the desert? What would be the modern equivalent of manna in the desert?

Back to the gospels and the parable of the fig tree (Lk 13:6–9): what causes a fig tree not to bloom? What kinds of fig trees are there and what did the one Jesus was talking about look like? Look at the passion and death of Jesus from the various gospel accounts: what type of terrain would Jesus have walked on while carrying the cross? From what type of tree did the wood for the cross come? What kinds of trees are there in Israel that would have been strong enough to hold a person?

Using the naturalist intelligence makes us look at our faith teaching in a different way. We have to delve into areas we normally don't consider, and see the things we often take for granted. Let's look at some more exercises using the naturalist intelligence. It's time for an immersion in nature.

GEARS

Have the group pretend they are a machine, and each person plays a small moving part. Add sound. Encourage the group to run as long as they can. Discuss what occurs. What does this say about community and about church?

GROWTH IN FAITH

Prepare a picture of a tree, from roots to top. Be as detailed or as simple as you like. Prepare cards on the tree's parts: trunk, leaves, roots, branches, and so on. Again, be as detailed or as simple as you want. Prepare cards with different elements important to our growth in faith: a solid foundation, our relationship with God and with other people, prayer, and so on. Match these elements to the tree parts. Mix the cards and ask the group to put them in the correct place. How are we like a tree? How do the parts of the tree match our growth in faith? What other things can we learn from our comparison with a tree?

BIRTH OF JESUS

Have several items from the Christmas story, such as swaddling clothes, myrrh, wool, census books, reservation form for a hotel, and straw. Mix these up in a basket. Ask a child to come forward and choose one item from the basket, then have them analyze the object: where does this item fit in the Christmas story? Does this object come straight from nature, or is it man-made? What qualities does it have in common with the other objects? What makes it unique? What might be the equivalent of this object today? Repeat this process, asking a different youngster to answer the questions above for each one of the objects.

THE HEALING OF JESUS

Make cards that illustrate the healing miracles of Jesus, such as the ten lepers, the woman who was bleeding, the man lowered through the ceiling, and so on. Gather objects that would represent the various aliments in the healings, along with objects that would be used to heal people of these ailments. Then have the group match the objects to the healings.

Discuss these healings. How are these ailments treated in our contemporary world? Would Jesus use miracles to heal people today? What objects in the ailment and what objects in the cures are the same? Which are different? Continue with questions that encourage an understanding of Jesus' healing ministry.

TERRARIUM TERRAIN

Have the children create individual terrariums that show parts of the Holy Land or the early Christian world. Use a plastic two-liter soda container or clear glass jar. After the youngsters have determined what area they would like to portray, begin to gather the materials necessary for the terrarium (if these cannot easily be found in nature you can use representations). Don't forget to consider plants, soil, animals, and any other distinctive features. Assemble the terrarium. Finish the project by putting a label on the outside of the container that identifies the area. If it was taken from Scripture, add a verse or two describing the area.

STICKY FAITH

Have each participant take two pieces of paper. Hold them together. Do they stick? Now have them wet each piece of paper and again hold them together. Do they stick now? Can you peel them apart? How easy or difficult is this? Can you slide them apart? Let the pages dry in a warm place and see what happens.

Our faith is like the pieces of paper. When we are spiritually dry because we haven't nurtured our faith, we can't be in union with others and God. But when we nurture our faith and immerse ourselves in it, we have real stick-to-it-ness. We must keep nurturing our faith or it will dry up, and we will once again lose contact with God.

WALKS WITH GOD

Take a walk outside and look for shapes (circle, triangle, square, etc.) in nature. What are the shapes in our faith?

On another walk, find things in nature beginning with each letter of the alphabet. Make a similar list for things or people in our faith, and compare the two lists. Have the group walk for a certain number of steps, then stop and record what they have seen and heard. Have the group walk for a certain number of steps and ask them to listen to God as they walk, then record what they have seen and heard. Repeat this activity as often as you'd like.

ORIENTING YOURSELF TO GOD

In your meeting space or another area, set up ten stations. Think of ten different clues that will be at the various stations. Each clue will represent something that relates to a particular quality of God. Pace the steps between each station, then use this information to write out a set of instructions for each station. In the instructions, use directions such as this: "Go North 20 paces, go West 15 paces, Turn, go North 5 paces."

Have the children do the course individually or in teams. At the start each person or team receives a compass, paper and pencil, and a set of instructions. The person or groups may start the course at different places. After each has finished the course, take some time to find out what was difficult, what was easy, what they learned about God, and most important, what qualities of God they discovered.

The naturalist intelligence is in love with nature. It enables people to see the order and structure of the universe quite easily. People who are strong in this intelligence make connections between patterns and innately sense what is shared in groups.

These are the children in your classrooms who like to collect and organize things. Remember our story about Clyde, the horse, in the beginning of the book? While Clyde was running out of the forest, the naturalist intelligence person would stop to see the trees, smell the flowers, and study the bugs. He or she would put the ogre under scrutiny, and tell Clyde about the strengths common to his breed.

Introduce exercises for the naturalist intelligence into your classroom, and you will be surprised by the order that reigns and the wonders of nature you discover.

CHAPTER VIII

Intrapersonal

I pray that God may give you a spirit of wisdom and revelation…so that, with the eyes of your heart enlightened, you may know what is the hope to which he has called you, what are the riches of his glorious inheritance among the saints, and what is the immeasurable greatness of his power for us who believe, according to the working of his great power.

Ephesians 1:17–19

We've all known quiet people. They might have been in our religious education classes or in adult formation groups. We've seen them in our families and in our parish. Perhaps our first inclination is to label all quiet people as shy, or think that they are off in some other realm. But then they say something that blows us away.

Being quiet is one of the characteristics of intrapersonal intelligence. Gardner defines it as the knowledge of the internal aspects of self such as feelings, emotional responses, self-reflection, and an intuitive sense about spiritual realities. People highly developed in this intelligence are good at focusing, concentrating, and thinking things through. They have a strong sense of self, are confident, and enjoy working alone. They are keenly aware of their strengths and abilities.

Both of my children seem to be very much in touch with who they are as well as with their strengths and weaknesses. I, on the other hand, am often caught up in wanting to play the guitar as well as someone else, or paint better than someone else. On the other hand, I often downgrade my own abilities, feeling they are not as good other people's. All in all, I don't have a clear picture of my strengths and weaknesses. My children, however, know what they do well and take pride in it; they also know what they are unable to do and are not afraid to ask for help. This shows a strong intrapersonal intelligence.

I once used the the story of Jack and the Beanstalk in an adult formation class, to illustrate the concept of values. Each group was working on a different aspect of the story using a different intelligence. At one point, I noticed that the group assigned to intrapersonal intelligence was struggling—except for one person who was quiet. I came over to the group and offered a few suggestions. Then the quiet one spoke. "That's a good suggestion," she said, "and I have a few more." On that note I moved on to another group.

The time came for the groups to make their presentations. There were skits and songs and game shows, and then it was time for the intrapersonal group to present their interpretation. Each person in the group had assumed the persona of one of the characters in the story: the mother, Jack, the man who sold him the beans, the giant's wife, and the giant.

The presentation began with Jack's mother sitting alone and crying. She then looked up at the audience: "I've tried so hard since my husband died. It's so difficult. First there was some money and then there was none. I want to be a good mother to Jack, but with my belly hungry and so much work to do, sometimes I take it out on him. I yell because God doesn't seem to hear me. That's the bottom line. I don't feel God hears me."

Then Jack appeared, pacing the floor. "I know my mother loves me, but sometimes I just don't feel loved. She's so busy so much of the time and I try to help when I can but it's never enough. And when we are both hungry, we can't seem to hear each other. When she gave me the cow to sell, I was determined to do my best, but then I met the man with the beans. He offered me hope. I don't have any hope that things can be better, and so I took his offer. I wanted hope. My mother wanted money."

The man with the beans walked across the room. "I need to make a living. I barter, and when there's an opportunity to get more for my goods, I take it. Jack was that opportunity. Beans for a cow? Who ever heard of that? I think the boy would've taken anything. He was hungry for a change in his life. I was eager to give it to him because it would give me a change in mine. I sold that cow for one hundred dollars."

The giant's wife sat, sewing. "It's so hard being married to someone who controls you. He yells and tells me I'll never measure up. Sometimes he even hits me. I didn't want that poor boy to suffer the same fate I have these many years. People ask me why I don't leave. They don't understand; I wouldn't make it in the human world. And here in the giant's world, there is no other way to survive. So I stay with him. I'm not happy, but I do what I can to save others."

The giant pounced into the scene, snorting. "Do you know what it is like to be discriminated against? It's not fun. It's cruel. And so you learn how to defend yourself. A lot of times that defense comes with hurting others first so you won't get hurt. That's what I do with my wife. That's what I wanted to do with Jack. He didn't realize how lucky he was just to have a mother. She loves the poor bloke. I don't have anyone who loves me. I chase away love because I don't want to be hurt again. It makes me want to hurt people."

There was silence when the performance ended. No one had looked at the fairy tale in quite that light. The reasons why the characters might have acted the way they did came out in that presentation. This knowledge changed the group's understanding of the story; Jack and the Beanstalk would never be the same. It was now a means of teaching the importance of love to all people.

Asking the big questions

People with strong intrapersonal intelligence will look at the deeper picture not readily seen. They generally are not concerned about others' opinions. They are confident, self-reflective, and aware, and often they are able to express feelings in a variety of ways.

These people will get into someone's persona and question the reasons for various actions. You can try this with a Bible story, for instance, the Good Samaritan (Lk 10:30–37). What were the thoughts of the priest who passed by the injured man? The Levite? The Samaritan? The injured man himself? The innkeeper? How do we respond to this story as Christians? Are we able to forgive the priest and Levite? Can we comprehend the motivation of the Samaritan? How does this impact our understanding of the parable?

During a middle school session on Jesus' crucifixion, the group was having a difficult time determining what types of emotions might have been present in the crowd. So we stopped the lesson and played a game. I have a stack of cards on which are printed faces with a variety of emotions—boredom, anger, happiness, confusion, and so on. I had two volunteers from the group sit across from each other. One partner was to pick a card and make a face indicating the emotion on that card. The other person was to try and guess the emotion. After four emotions, I had them switch places. Soon we had several people wanting to try their hand at this. When we finally got back to the discussion about the crucifixion, the group had a much better understanding of the emotions that might have been present in the crowd at Calvary.

This type of exercise helps people get in touch with their emotions. It helps intrapersonal people express the range of their feelings. A variation of this is to take a prayer that is familiar and ask someone to say the prayer in the following ways—as if they are describing a mystery; really bored; reading a recipe; very nervous, terrified, or elated. This is a great way to show how prayer can cover the gamut of emotions. It's OK to be angry with God or to laugh with God or, even, to tell God a mystery.

One evening several years ago, I was walking past my son's room and I heard laughter. Since he had gone to bed at least an hour earlier and the bedside light was out, I was surprised by the sound. I peered into his room. His eyes were closed, and a smile played on his lips.

"Nathaniel," I called out tentatively. "Are you all right?" His eyes flew open.

"Sure, Mom. Why?"

"I just heard someone laughing. Maybe you were dreaming."

"Oh, that. I wasn't dreaming. I was saying my prayers. I told a joke to God, and God just told me one even better."

This was prayer at its finest, sharing an intimately joyful relationship with your Maker.

Intrapersonal intelligence allows us to take what we are hearing and seeing and internalize it. What we take in, we make part of us. In a recent presentation to catechists, one catechist told of having a little boy in her class who never said a word, never contributed to a discussion, and never asked a question. When the teacher ran into the mother one day, she was surprised when the mom started thanking her profusely. Puzzled, the catechist asked why.

The mother answered, "Because my son comes home after every class and gives us a blow by blow account of what you covered. You are doing so much and giving him so many experiences, I am just so grateful."

Dumfounded, the catechist thanked the mother and then did some reflecting. It seemed that this child was like a sponge, soaking up anything and everything, so much so he was able to teach another.

Internalizing our faith is very important. Otherwise there is the danger that our faith stays on the surface, and develops little, if any, real meaning in our lives. In the Letter of James we are cautioned:

> What good is it, my brothers and sisters, if you say you have faith but do not have works? Can faith save you? If a brother or sister is

naked and lacks daily food, and one of you says to them, "Go in peace; keep warm and eat your fill," and yet you do not supply their bodily needs, what is the good of that? So faith by itself, if it has no works, is dead.

—James 2:14–17

Only when we internalize our faith can it be translated into works. Only when we finally hear and take into our hearts what it is we believe are we able to grow in our faith. Intrapersonal intelligence helps us get in touch with our feelings, and emotions, which can nourish faith in our hearts.

⏱ *How can you make use of intrapersonal intelligence in your faith formation sessions?* You've already seen some ways, and now here are eight suggestions to take you further. As Margaret Sackville, poet and children's author, writes, "Great imaginations are apt to work from hints and suggestions, and a single moment of emotion is sometimes sufficient to create a masterpiece." Let these words inspire you to create your own activities as you go along.

IN THE AUDIENCE

Select two children from the group. Ask them to pretend that they are watching a biblical event. Have each child react to the event, and see if the rest of the group can guess what they are feeling.

MOUNTAIN OR BEACH?

Ask the children in your group to consider if they are more like a mountain or more like a beach. If they are more like a mountain, they go to one side of the room; more like a beach, to the other side. Then have them pair up and discuss why they made that choice. Give more pairings to the group, such as breakfast/supper, giver/receiver/, television/radio, and so on and follow the same procedure What does this say about the different characteristics of God's creation?

APPOINTMENT WITH DEATH

If possible, visit a cemetery. Have the children take note of some of the inscriptions on the tombstones, especially the years and the names. Let everyone spend some time quietly walking around. When you return (or at the cemetery, if it is a nice day) give the children some paper or poster board and have them create their own tombstone. On one side have them plan what it would say if they died today; on the other, what would be written if they died of old age. Invite them to discuss what they felt and what our faith has to say about death.

THE MANDARIN

This exercise, of unknown origin, is for preteens, teens, and adults. Variations have been made of it for as long as I have been in ministry.

Gather the group in a circle around a single lit candle. Together you are going to decide on the life of a human being. In your hand you hold eleven envelopes. You open the first and read:

Envelope #1. A candle flickers. Its flame dances with life, with a life more delicate than the breath of life in people. The astrological heavens reinforce the candle's importance. A blood red moon joins Venus, in the third quadrant, linking this fragile flame to the life of a man. In a remote village of northern China, a Mandarin, the village elder, doesn't even dream that his life will cease if the candle is snuffed out. If you blow out the candle, the Mandarin dies. But now the heavens change a bit. Jupiter comes into the fourth quadrant in direct relationship to the moon and Venus. The Mandarin's life is still linked with the candle flame but so is something else. If the flame is extinguished, earth will have 200 years of peace and prosperity. Do you blow out the candle and bring peace and prosperity to earth for 200 years at the cost of the Mandarin's life?

Discuss and then vote. The majority rules. If yes, open Envelope #2. If no, Envelope #3.

Envelope #2. The Mandarin is dead. Peace and prosperity have come to the world, but it is the peace and prosperity of the cemetery. When one person says he can decide who has the right to live and die, then any person can claim that right. Unfortunately this was not the only candle linked astrologically with someone's life. Every person on earth had a candle linked to someone else. When you voted to blow out the candle, everyone made the same decision you did. With one breath, every man, woman, and child on earth was killed. Peace?

Envelope #3. The Mandarin goes on living, but all his life he's been a dedicated communist. His fondest dream is that one day communism will cover the world. He believes this will bring peace and prosperity to the world. You can still blow out the candle and bring 200 years of peace and prosperity at the price of this man's life. Do you blow it out?

Discuss. Vote and you must have a complete consensus. If yes, open Envelope #4, if no, Envelope #5.

Envelope #4. Twenty years ago the Mandarin died mysteriously. We are now living in a world of peace and prosperity unparalleled in human history. This has happened because one government now rules the world. It rules with an iron hand. It demands control over every aspect of its citizens' lives. When you voted to kill the Mandarin because he was of the wrong political party, because his views did not agree with yours, then in effect you were saying others have the right to do the same thing. So we now have peace and prosperity, but bought at the price of a government that watches over every move you make and kills those who do not agree totally with it.

Envelope #5. The Mandarin still lives, but is an outcast. Some villagers have brought evidence he has stolen village funds that were supposed to be used for badly needed food and medicine. Even though he is hated by the whole village, the Mandarin is still happy to be alive. He looks forward to seeing the sun rise every morning. Do you blow out the candle and buy peace and prosperity at the cost of his life?

Discuss. Vote and the majority rules this time. If yes, Envelope #6, if no, Envelope #7.

Envelope #6. The Mandarin has died. Some say he died of a broken heart because the village people had rejected him. This was especially unfortunate because a few days after his burial, new evidence was found to show that he had not stolen any of the missing money. An uneasy peace and prosperity hovers over the world. It is uneasy because of a group called the Deciders. If a person is suspected of conduct disruptive to peace and prosperity, the Deciders will have him or her killed immediately. This way things are very peaceful but the population continues to get smaller and smaller.

Envelope #7. The Mandarin is still alive, friends with everyone because the money that was missing was found. He was innocent. But the Mandarin is not happy. His wife had died and all the joy in his life is gone. Nothing brings him happiness anymore. He was so close to his wife that he wishes he were dead so he could be with her. He is completely depressed and sick of living. Do you blow the candle out?

Discuss. Vote. You must have a consensus. If yes, read Envelope #8, if not read Envelope #9.

Envelope #8. The Mandarin is dead. Peace and prosperity have come to the whole world. One of the reasons why is that the depressed and the mentally ill are no longer allowed to live. They are thought to mess up society. Suicide is also encouraged among the depressed and the mentally ill or challenged. People feel that anyone who wants to die is probably no good to society.

Envelope #9. The Mandarin is happy again. He has realized if he really loved his wife, he would not continue to grieve over her death. He again enjoys life, but, unfortunately his age is catching up with him. He's come down with a painful lung infection which has him near death and in constant pain. Yet he's still happy to be alive. Do you blow out the candle?

Discuss the pros and cons. Vote with the majority ruling. If yes, read Envelope #10, if no read Envelope #11.

Envelope #10. The old man is dead because the candle has been blown out. Peace and prosperity have come to the whole world, but at a tremendous price. We have no more homes for the aged, no more hospitals, no more invalids who are a drain on society and the economy. Mercy killing has become a common place thing. Only the strongest are allowed to live. The old and the sick are put away for good.

Envelope #11. The old man somehow pulled himself together and survived. During his illness, he had a vision of a plan to bring peace and prosperity to the whole world through the recognition of each person's unique value and the universal brother and sisterhood of men and women. The old Mandarin walked to Peking to take his plan to the leaders of China. They in turn took it to the United Nations, all nations on earth accepted it, bringing for the first time in the history of our planet, an age of universal peace and prosperity.

Discuss feelings and reactions. This is an excellent exercise for determining what individuals are valuing and thinking.

MOVIES AND GOD

Take a group to see a movie suitable for their age. Afterward or at your next session together, discuss the movie. What was the theme? What character did you like the most? Least? Was this movie true to life? Why or why not? What character would God play? What lesson is the movie teaching? What changes would you make to the movie? This is an excellent exercise because it allows young people to consider their faith in light of popular culture.

TIME TO INTERVIEW

Set up a time to interview your class about a topic you are studying or have studied. This could be further expanded to talk about current events as they relate to our faith. The person interviewed should answer questions honestly and openly. He or she can pass on any question if they are uncomfortable answering it, and can end the interview at any time by simply saying, "Thanks for the interview."

MY BIBLICAL JOURNAL

Have the children pretend they have been put into a Bible story as one of the characters. Ask them to write about what is happening in the story and how they feel about it: who are the people they are meeting and how they feel about them; what they are doing in the story, and how they feel about that; and so on. Ask some of the children to read their accounts to the class.

TIGER TALK

Ask each person to imagine a mirror in front of them. Have them think of something they don't like to do or are afraid of doing. Tell them to talk to themselves in the mirror and try to convince themselves that they can do whatever it is they don't like or are afraid of. Tell them they are free to shout at themselves, talk quietly, or express themselves in whatever way they wish. Be prepared, because the room will get noisy!

When the talking is done, discuss how important it is to build confidence in ourselves. Talk about how God made us to be good, confident people, yet too often we let time and circumstances destroy that confidence. Ask the children to talk about what they felt in front of the mirror. What did they learn about themselves?

Sister Jose Hobday teaches Native American ritual and spirituality in lectures and workshops throughout the world. One of the prayers which she introduces is the hug prayer, which was taught to Sr. Hobday by her mother. I have come to find that it is a beautiful prayer to teach to people with intrapersonal intelligence. It puts their reflection and introspection in the hands of God. When you wonder if you have the strength to reach out to all the different intelligence, I invite you to use this prayer.

Become aware of God present. Now put your arms around yourself. Cuddle your body. Hold yourself like you would hold a baby. Once you have a good hold of yourself, close your eyes and begin to rock. Keep doing it. Remember you are God's child and God understands and holds you close, just the way you are holding yourself. Just bathe in the fact that God loves you very much.

People with intrapersonal intelligence are the spiritual counselors, the gurus, the people with detailed, accurate self-knowledge. They are the people with the ability to understand their own emotions, goals, and intentions. They have the ability to take personal knowledge and use it to guide behavior and decisions. They are our leaders.

CHAPTER IX

Interpersonal

The Lord said to Abram, after Lot had separated from him, "Raise your eyes now, and look from the place where you are, northward and south-ward and eastwards and westwards; for all the land that you see I will give to you and to your offspring for ever. I will make your offspring like the dust of the earth; so that if one can count the dust of the earth, your offspring also can be counted."

Genesis 13:14–17

.

In the book, *The Magic Wall,* Judy Varga tells the story of Rudolf I of Austria, a humble and popular ruler in the 1300s. The castle she speaks of is still standing today. It was a castle unlike all the other stark, forbidding castles that surrounded it. This one was sunlit and cheerful in a lush valley, and it had no wall. Daily the king and queen walked among the people and joined in their activities.

One day a neighboring king came and told this kind ruler that his castle was not royal enough, and that he should have a wall around it to protect it from his enemies. And so the good king built a wall around his castle in an effort to make it more royal and to protect him from his enemies. The wall, however, also kept the king and queen away from the people, however, and the people grew suspicious and unfriendly. The once happy castle became a castle of dissent.

When the good king saw what havoc and distrust the wall had brought to his kingdom, he went out and began to tear it down. When the people saw this, they joined in the dismantling. Once the wall was down, the kingdom returned to its happy ways.

When the neighboring king passed through again, he was horrified. He threatened to attack and take the good king's kingdom.

"I don't need your kind of walls," said the good king. "I have walls but only my enemies can see them. My watchtowers are higher than any king's, but I don't need soldiers to man them."

The neighboring king didn't know what to make of this since he could see no walls. But when he looked up he saw that while they were talking the people of the village had formed a wall around the castle; the hunters manned the hillside "towers." The neighboring king bid the good king goodbye, finally realizing that the wall and the towers this good king had, made of love and trust, were stronger and longer lasting than any made of stone.

This is the power of interpersonal intelligence. Interpersonal people have the ability to detect and respond appropriately to the moods, motivations, and desires of others. Like the good king, they are in harmony with other people. Gardner points out that they have the ability to work cooperatively with others in a group as well as the ability to communicate both verbally and non-verbally with other people. These are the therapists, the salespeople, the teachers, the politicians, and religious leaders. They are the people who call others to community.

Rabbi Saul Rubin, a leader in community building says, "We have stories to tell, stories that provide wisdom about the journey of life. What more have we to give one another than our truth about our human adventure as honestly and as openly as we know how?" The interpersonal intelligence people are the ones ready to share the stories and to hear the stories of others.

Several years ago, I started helping out at the Shalom Catholic Worker House in Kansas City, Kansas, cooking and cleaning two days a week. Every Wednesday, once the beds were made, the clothes washed, and the bathrooms cleaned, Mary K Meyer, the director of the house, and I would sit down and share a cup of tea. Some days we would sit in quiet, saying little, if anything. Most days, we talked about our week or about books we were reading, or about the lives of the people who came and went from the house.

Sometimes Mary K would reminisce about the early years of her life. I listened to this peace-loving activist tell how during World War II, she led a group called the Flying Tigers whose job it was to keep track of the war events overseas. She'd tell of silly pranks she and her friends would play on Halloween, and of a religious revival held in a tent in a neighboring town and how it changed her life. I shared with her the difficulties I was having with my family or my apprehensions about a particular religious education program.

Through talking with Mary K about our life experiences I learned that I didn't have to be perfect. The dichotomy in my life was OK as long as I was working to make things different, better, more in line with what I believed. She taught me God is a real force who cares about my trivial concerns as well as my serious ones. She taught me one of the most important lessons in my life, that loss is inevitable but what's important is what you do with loss. Loss has to help you grow and change or it would have a power it doesn't deserve.

Community building

It was in the simple sharing of those life experiences that I was able to grow. That's what a person with interpersonal intelligence is called to do—share, compare, relate, cooperate, interview, and teach. They are called to "climb into" another person's life.

Albert Einstein said, "The individual, if left alone from birth, would remain primitive and beastlike in his thoughts and feelings to a degree that we can hardly conceive. The individual is what he is and has the significance that he has not so much in virtue of this individuality but rather as a member of a great human community, which directs his material and spiritual existence from the cradle to the grave."

If we didn't have people with strong interpersonal intelligence, we would be left to flounder, remaining beastlike in thought and feeling. When you look at today's society, with its lack of community and interaction, you can see the lack of emphasis on interpersonal intelligence. We need to nurture this intelligence in our schools, in our homes, and in our neighborhoods if we hope to change the escalating violence and hatred present in our world today.

My family likes to have parties. Whether we have an occasion to celebrate or not, we enjoy getting together with people to share food and drink, talking and games. We keep things as simple as possible, and don't do much by way of preparation or clean-up. Yet it seems that so many people these days are reluctant to get together with others.

Interpersonal people encourage such gatherings. It is an opportunity for people to be together, to share, to laugh, to cry, to fight. How many of us have said that the only time we see some people is at weddings and funerals? Could it be that we are not willing to make the effort to meet with one another outside of such events?

The interpersonal intelligence is good at understanding people, leading others, organizing, communicating, and mediating conflicts. Often, after a community has been formed, the interpersonal intelligence is able to better mediate in conflicts. "There is a fantasy abroad," says M. Scott Peck, author of *The Road Less Traveled*. "Simply stated, it goes like this: If we can resolve our conflicts then someday we shall be able to live together in community. Could it be that we have it totally backward? And that the real dream should be: if we can live together in community then someday we shall be able to resolve our conflicts?"

We know how important it is to mediate conflict. More and more in our world we are faced with angry people who choose violent solutions to problems. If we could develop our interpersonal intelligence and use it to promote stronger communities and a more widespread sense of belonging, then perhaps our conflicts could better be dealt with and resolved.

The children whose strength is interpersonal intelligence are often the ones who will note when someone is missing from class. These are the children who are good at listening and communicating, and are sensitive to the moods and feelings of others. Often they can figure out other people's motives and intentions. They are the first to give someone the benefit of the doubt. These young people enjoy discussing solutions to problems and brainstorming about projects. They like teamwork.

Interpersonal intelligence calls us to make sure there is a community component in our faith formation sessions. This is an essential ingredient in the Montessori classroom, as well. Here the children are encouraged to develop a sense of ownership and responsibility. They become sensitive to each other and tolerant of each other's learning capabilities. Because they see their classroom as belonging to them, the children not only take care of the room but of each other. As religious educators, we have much to learn from this approach to community building.

In your own group, encourage the children to take good care of whatever materials your might use. Talk about the group as being a community and about what is entailed in being community—namely, the aspects of care and responsibility. Once you have established a communal atmosphere, the children's interpersonal intelligence will enhance it and help it grow.

 Here are some exercises to help your children grow in community.

RUMORS

This is based on the children's game called Telephone. Choose six children and ask them to leave the room. Then, create a brief story with the children who remain. Use specific details—names, dates, places, and so on. Call one of the six back into the room, and tell the story to him or her. Then another of the six comes back into the room, and the first person tells the story to the new person, with no help from the group. The process is repeated until all six have returned and heard the story.

The last person to hear the story writes it down as he or she heard it. Compare this account to the original story. As a group, discuss how much change has occurred in the story. What does this say about our communication with others? How does communication impact community, both positively and negatively?

WALKING THE LINE

Place masking tape on the floor in various directions or in a continuous circle. Direct the group to walk on the line, following each other one by one, placing one foot in front of the other so their feet stay on the masking tape. Make the activity more difficult by having them walk while balancing a book on their heads or carrying a glass of water without spilling. This helps them learn to work together, encourage each other, and concentrate.

GROUP PARABLE

Have the group write a parable together. Tell them they will each have a few minutes to write part of the story. Have one child begin the writing and work for one to two minutes. He or she then passes it on to the next person to write, and so on. The finished work can be illustrated, again with everyone working together.

THE PRODIGAL SON

Assign the children to groups of four or five, and have them design a model of the area where the prodigal son story takes place. Where were the pigs? Where was the father's house? Where did the brother work? Where was the gambling? Have them do a presentation of the project.

THIS IS YOUR FAITH

Ask the group to devise a board game or action game around a concept of faith or an aspect of church history. Be sure to include rules, materials, and the purpose of the game.

WHO ARE YOU, EXACTLY?

Prepare sheets of paper with questions about things people would like to know about each other. Be sure and include questions about beliefs. Make sure there are enough sheets for every child in the group. Pair off everyone in the group and have them take turns asking each other the questions on their sheets. Allow enough time for them to explore friendships with each other.

WHAT DO I DO?

On several index cards, write out a moral dilemma or a problem that is common to the age level of the children in your group. Have the youngsters work together in small groups to resolve these situations. Afterwards, the groups can present their work to the larger group.

MINI-EXPERT

Let each child pick a concept that the group has studied and prepare a five minute mini-lesson on it. Have them teach it to the rest of the class. This is great as a review for the end of the year.

Loneliness can be a difficult cross to bear. We feel cut off from people, as though we don't belong. When we as educators encourage the growth of community and the development of interpersonal intelligence, we answer the need in everyone's heart to be part of a community. We help people realize they are not alone, that even in their darkest moments they are connected with others and, above all, connected with God.

When we nurture community with those with whom we work, they come to know the meaning of the words of sixteenth-century mystic Julian of Norwich: "We were all created at the same time; and in our creation we were knit and oned to God. By this we are kept as luminous and noble as when we were created. By the force of this precious oneing we love, seek, praise, thank, and endlessly enjoy our Creator."

CHAPTER X

Existential

Then Amos answered Amaziah, "I am no prophet, nor a prophet's son; but I am a herdsman, and a dresser of sycamore trees, and the Lord took me from following the flock, and the Lord said to me, 'Go, prophesy to my people Israel.' Now therefore hear the word of the Lord."

Amos 7:14–16

Whenever I see the evening news, I never fail to ask the big questions. Why does God allow mud slides in Guatemala that killed hundreds? Why do people see murder as the only resolution to their problems? Despite knowing the facts, why do some people continue to abuse the earth? Children, too, ask the big questions. Where did Daddy go when he died? What is heaven like? What is evil? Who is God?

According to Gardner, existential intelligence is the sensitivity and capacity to tackle profound questions about human existence, such as, what is the meaning of life, why do we die, and how did we get here. Rainer Maria Rilke, one of the great German lyric poets of modern times, wrote, "You must give birth to your images. They are the future waiting to be born. Fear not the strangeness you feel. The future must enter into

96

you long before it happens." When I first read this quote, I felt it was speaking directly to people with existential intelligence. It was saying how important it is to grapple with these questions because without the grappling there could not be the reality.

A few years ago, I was working with a group of catechists, showing them how they could use multiple intelligence in their religion sessions. We had gone through the first eight intelligence, and had just begun existential intelligence. Since this intelligence has only recently been identified, there was little material about how to incorporate it into the classroom in a practical way—let alone in faith formation programs. So I turned inward to the Spirit and took a leap.

I explained to the group that what we were about to do might bring up some serious questions, and some deep feelings might surface, but if they were willing, we would try. They gave their assent and we began. First, we would decide on a disaster, either from the past or present. Since the September 11, 2001 attack had recently occurred and feelings about it were still raw, I encouraged the group to choose another situation, and they settled on the sinking of the Titanic.

I then asked the group to act out this event, beginning with the shipbuilder extolling the virtues of the boat to the group. The presentation continued as the people starting out on the cruise dined and danced and enjoyed the voyage. Not everyone participated in this revelry, however, as staff and lower-class passengers were restricted below deck. Then came the iceberg and the horror of not having enough lifeboats, of people freezing in the arctic waters, of watching loved ones die before their eyes.

I then asked the group to act out the disaster with different circumstances and a different outcome. For instance, the shipbuilder had insisted that there be enough lifeboats for everyone on board. There was still dining and dancing but there were no locks on the third class passageways. Thus, when the iceberg hit, the staff and passengers in the lower levels quickly rose to help as much as they could, urging calm in a sea of panic. As a consequence, almost everyone survived.

I looked out at a sea of drained but happy faces as I began a discussion of both presentations and what implications they had for our faith. The catechists talked about acting from a Christian outlook of love for all people. They talked about thinking of the other person. They discussed prejudice and how it affects our actions. They shared their thoughts about feeling at peace with death, and about life after death. They talked about judgment.

At the end of the session, several people stayed behind to discuss the impact which this last activity had on them. "I need to look at these questions," said one young teacher. "I want to put them off, but doing that is reflected in my behavior. This activity really helped me to see what I was doing."

"I agree," a man added. "I felt so powerless after the attacks of September 11th. After doing this exercise, I feel a sense of power in myself, in my faith, and in God. I feel that I can make an impact in life because so much of what I do hinges on what another person does or doesn't do. We're all in this together."

When we began the exercise, I thought I might be treading on volatile territory. Instead we were asking the big questions, helping people consider them and empower themselves in that way. Existential intelligence enables us to do that.

Dealing with life's pain

For a number of years I worked in a parish located in a small town in northern Minnesota. As part of our ministry, we ran an outreach center called The Rest Room where teens were able to come, have something to drink and eat, play games, and socialize. The center was open every Friday and Saturday night and regularly drew a crowd that included not only Catholic teens but those from other denominations.

One Saturday night was especially busy. Kids were all around, some talking in twosomes, others giggling and playing games in groups of four or more. The noise level was loud and spirits were high. Suddenly the senior class president at the high school came through the front door. His eyes were frantic and his speech was garbled.

"Wes, what's wrong?" I asked, taking his hand.

He pulled at my hand. "Come! It's terrible! A cat, hit by a truck!" I followed him outside, others following us. "See!" He pointed in the distance. "He's there, dying. We have to help him!"

I strained my eyes to look. "I'm sorry, Wes, but I don't see anything."

"You have to! Can't you see? It's in pain!"

"I can't, Wes. Why don't you come in and sit a while, calm down, and we'll give animal control a call." I started to tug him back toward the door.

"No!" he screeched and with that he ran off up the street, away from the center.

I couldn't leave the youth center unattended, so I asked a few of his classmates to go after him and make sure he was all right. They did, and returned a little later saying that he had calmed down, especially once he saw there had been no cat. His classmates decided that bed was the best place for him, so they left him at his house and returned to the center.

I didn't see Wes on Sunday, which wasn't unusual since he attended a different church. Monday morning, however, I was awakened early by a call from the father of one of the seniors. Wes had shot and killed himself on the steps of the church that morning.

I was devastated. Was there anything I could have done? Was the incident of the cat a cry for help? I tortured myself with these questions until the phone calls began. One after another Wes's classmates were calling because they couldn't come to terms with what had happened.

The funeral was held the next day. I stood by the side of the casket as the kids went by, each stopping for a hug, overcome with grief. I could say nothing. I could only hurt with them. Why does God let something like this happen?

The next week during our confirmation session, the planned program was thrown to the winds. Instead we dealt with questions such as, why does something like this happen? Why did Wes feel so desperate? What is it that keeps people going on in hope? And the questions went on.

None of the questions were met with pat answers. Each question had to be answered by the individual. This class was grappling with the big questions of life and death. They were thrust into using their existential intelligence without realizing it. Had I known more about this intelligence at the time, perhaps I might have been able to guide their questions and reflections in different ways.

I do remember that one of the teens showed great existential intelligence. He listened to his classmates, reflected, and talked about what had happened. He later asked to read something at the prayer service that we held for Wes. He read this, from the Greek playwright Aeschylus: "How dear you will be to me then, you nights of anguish. Why didn't I kneel more deeply to accept you, inconsolable sisters, and, kneeling, love myself in your loosened hair? How we squander our hours of pain." He ended with his own words: "Don't be afraid of the hurt. Let it come. Make it a part of you. Question. Listen. Love." When he sat down, I could almost see the healing process begin.

Existential intelligence includes the likes of Aristotle, Confucius, Einstein, Emerson, Plato, Socrates, and of course, Jesus, as well as many of the saints, such as Thomas Aquinas, Elizabeth Ann Seton, and Teresa of Avila. It includes those people who cause us to think beyond the box, to think beyond the pain, to think beyond the joy. It causes us to think about eternity.

Now, how in the world do we integrate this intelligence with our religious education program? Here are eight suggestions to help you get started.

DESERTED CITY

Each young person is asked to think about their house and their neighborhood. A disaster has occurred and the place must be abandoned.

They are allowed to take only one object with them, one which will help them grow in their faith. What do they choose and why?

THE BIG QUESTION

Divide the class into small groups, and give each group a piece of paper. Allow each youngster two minutes to write down his or her answer to this question: who is God? Pass the paper around so that each person in the group can write an answer to that question. When everyone has had an opportunity to write, one of the children in the group reads what has been written in random order. Discussion then takes place on what has been written about God.

ON THE FLOOR

Use the following directions for a time of quiet reflection. Lie on your back (or sit quietly) with your eyes closed. Relax your entire body, starting with your feet and moving up, one body part at a time, to your head. Now ask yourself one question you have always wondered about. Listen to your heart. Each time your mind starts to wander, gently pull it back to the question and to your heart. After a time, open your eyes. Write down what you heard.

AFRAID OF GHOSTS

Have the children think of someone close to them who has died or to think of a figure from history. Imagine they are alone at home and this individual comes to visit them. Ask: how would you react? What questions might you ask the ghost? What might the ghost respond?

HEAVEN AND HELL

Ask the children to write down or draw their concept of heaven and of hell. Tell them to be as specific as possible: how would time in each place be spent? What would determine your presence in either place?

How has your concept of both places changed as you have grown? How does it differ or how is it the same as Scripture references to heaven and hell?

ME AND MY PET

Where do pets go when they die? Using various materials, have the class create the place where pets go when they die. If the general consensus is that their life simply ends here, show that. If the group believes in something else, describe that. Be as detailed as possible.

WHY DID GOD MAKE YOU?

Give each person a sheet of paper. Have the class number their papers from one through five. Next to each number, ask them to give a reason why God made us. Once that is done, ask them to write down how the reasons God made them as individuals might change the way they live their lives. Tell them to be as specific as possible.

QUOTABLES

Take a quote from a famous person or from the Bible. Have the children write, illustrate, prepare a radio broadcast, or another means of expression to explain the quote from their viewpoint. The quote can be linked to what is being studied in religion class. For instance, if you are studying prayer, consider these words from John Donne: "I throw myself down in my chamber, and I call in and invite God and his angels thither. And when they are there, I neglect God and his angels for the noise of a file, for the rattling of a coach, for the whining of a door."

In his letter to the Ephesians, the apostle Paul writes:

God has made known to us the mystery of his will, according to his good pleasure that he set forth in Christ, as a plan for the fullness of time, to gather up all things in him, things in heaven and things on earth. In Christ we have also obtained an inheritance, having been destined according to the purpose of him who accomplishes all things according to his counsel and will.

Ephesians 1:9–11

Don't we all have to consider God's plan for our lives? When we challenge those with existential intelligence to consider the truths of our faith, we invite them and us to a deeper faith. When we dare to let them question, we enable ourselves to grow because we too must explore the questions and the answers. It helps all of us consider why we believe what we believe.

CHAPTER XI

Let's Get Specific

Rejoice always, pray without ceasing, give thanks in all circumstances; for this is the will of God in Christ Jesus for you. Do not quench the Spirit. Do not despise the words of prophets, but test everything; hold fast to what is good; abstain from every form of evil. May the God of peace himself sanctify you entirely; and may your spirit and soul and body be kept sound and blameless at the coming of our Lord Jesus Christ. The one who calls you is faithful, and he will do this.

1 Thessalonians 5:16–24

This passage always encourages me to take the risks involved in trying new things. You might even say that it is the blueprint for how a class about faith should be planned.

Notice that the first part talks about being joyful, prayerful, and thankful. God knows we can be joyful, prayerful, and thankful when everything is going well, but when we do take a risk and things go wrong, can we still be joyful, prayerful, and thankful? Note that the reading uses the words "always," "without ceasing," and "in all circumstances."

If we are going to make use of the multiple intelligences in our reli-

sessions, in our parishes, and in our homes, we have to remember these words. We must be joyful at all times, *"for this is the will of God…"*; this is what our faith is all about. We might have to work to bring out that joy because there have been many years when repressing this joy was our operational mode. We might have to get in touch with how we feel about our faith, and discover what about it brings us joy.

Next, we have to be prayerful. Nothing comes about without prayer. We have to be aware that God is present and among us, that God is ready, willing, and able to help if only we ask.

Finally, we must be thankful. Only from a heart filled with gratitude is love able to flow. It's like a cup filled to the brim, unable to hold anything more. Our thankfulness should fill us to the brim and spill over for others to feel.

"Do not quench the Spirit." This is especially true when working with multiple intelligence. We have to trust that what we are receiving in our hearts are ideas that are meant to be tried, risked, and shared. Every time I have trusted the Spirit, I have been blessed in ways I could never have planned. For example, there was the time we had a feet-washing ritual as a part of a service program for teenagers. The ceremony which I planned seemed to be going well. After all, I reflected, this was a bodily-kinesthetic activity and it was sure to be well-received. But I had not counted on one boy, who refused to have his feet washed.

More than that, I did not plan on another boy going with him to the restroom and returning a few minutes later, the obstinate boy willing now to wash his feet. Only after the session did I learn what had happened in the bathroom. The first boy had been too embarrassed to take off his shoes because he had holes in his socks. The second boy went into the bathroom, talked to the other, then changed socks with him. This was truly the Spirit at work. Do not restrain the Spirit.

"Do not despise the words of prophets." Their messages will come in many ways and from many different people. They may be spoken or drawn or prayed. Be alert. Don't ever start to think that only you have the words

of wisdom. Prophets know no age or schooling. They are the Lord's doing.

"Test everything…": *everything*. Put new ideas as well as old to the test. Always question. Look at everything you do with fresh eyes. In this way you will always be creating and fulfilling your call to be a co-creator with God.

"Hold fast to what is good; abstain from every form of evil." This doesn't mean we keep only what is good for us and throw away whatever we decide is evil. We have to be open to God working in us. We have to be open to new things that might cause us to be ill at ease. In short, we must stretch ourselves. We need to reach to heights we have never reached before. With an open heart, the presence of the Spirit, the words of Jesus, and the joyfulness of the Father, we can expect gentle yet powerful changes and growth not only in those we minster with, but most of all in ourselves.

This blueprint from Paul closes with a prayer that we be peaceful, holy, and ready to meet our Lord. The clincher is the last line: "The one who calls you is faithful, and he will do this." God calls us. God will do what we ask, and will always be there for us.

A thematic approach

Now that we have our blueprint and have looked at each of the intelligences, it is time to take one theme and see how the intelligence operate in a religion class or faith formation group.

Suppose our theme is Eucharist. In covering this topic our goals are to have participants 1. see Eucharist as central to the Catholic faith, 2. understand the meaning of the outward symbols of the sacrament, and 3. experience a sense of belonging to the larger Christian community through the Eucharist. Ultimately, we hope that with this type of a session everyone leaves with an experience and better understanding of the richness of the Eucharist.

We begin the lesson with an opening reflection (intrapersonal and logical-mathematical intelligence) about the history of our salvation. We relate how the history of our salvation is a long and beautiful one, and how, long before we can remember, long before records were kept, long before people were created, God loved us.

The reflection continues, taking participants through the Old Testament times and into Jesus' life and death. It ends as the light from Jesus—represented by a solitary candle placed in the center of the room—gives light to all the believers. Here one person lights a candle from the center candle, then gives the flame to another person, who then uses his or her candle to light someone else's, and so on. Thus we illustrate how salvation spreads.

On the heels of this reflection is a discussion (interpersonal and existential intelligence) about the reflection. What did this experience say about the Eucharist? Does this agree or disagree with what you know about Eucharist? How would you define Eucharist for someone else?

Next there is a presentation about Eucharist (verbal-linguistic, bodily-kinesthetic, and visual-spatial). During the presentation bread is made step-by-step. The participants are able to smell and feel the various ingredients in the bread. Each has an opportunity to knead the bread. When the bread is finished, the group is invited to participate in an early Christian worship service.

The room is darkened with only one candle lit, which symbolizes Christ among us. The participants are told to get comfortable in whatever way will help them worship, as did the early Christians (bodily-kinesthetic). Then they are invited to sing. Since there were no books in the early days of the church, the songs must be sung from memory (musical).

Following this, stories of Jesus are told. These too must come from memory since there were no books (verbal–linguistic). The participants can also talk about how Jesus has worked in their lives (intrapersonal, existential, and interpersonal). Then it is time for the petitions, prayers for those who could not be there (interpersonal).

Next comes the high point of our gathering, the blessing of the bread and the wine which is then shared with the group. The service draws to a close as the command is given to go forth with the good news and share it with others (interpersonal). The participants give a sign of peace to one another before leaving the gathering (bodily-kinesthetic).

So ends a session on the Eucharist that uses all of the intelligence in some form. You can see that many of the intelligence overlap; it is not difficult to employ them all in one session. The challenge comes in using those with which we may be less familiar, such as music, visual-spatial, existential, or bodily-kinesthetic. This, however, will vary with each teacher or group leader.

It is important that we take risks when we teach our faith. Only in this way can we grow and stretch in the ways that we can communicate the importance of faith to our children. The work we do in our classrooms, the risks we take, are a sign of our internal commitment to God and to our faith.

CHAPTER XII

Taking a Leap

I went down to the potter's house, and there he was working at his wheel. The vessel he was making of clay was spoiled in the potter's hand, and he reworked it into another vessel, as seemed good to him. Then the word of the Lord came to me: Can I not do with you, O house of Israel, just as this potter has done? says the Lord. Just like the clay in the potter's hand, so are you in my hand, O house of Israel.

Jeremiah 18:3–6

We come to know God first through our strongest intelligences. When we work to develop the other intelligence, our knowledge of God and of ourselves deepens.

Remember the story of the puddle fish in the introduction? In order to get to the sea, to the place where fish were meant to be, they had to take a leap into the river and ride the current out to the sea. Like the puddle fish, we must put aside our cowardice and fear and leap boldly forward to get to where we are meant to be.

The past chapters have talked about the different intelligences and the ways they can be used in a religious education setting. Time and again I have stressed the importance of being creative in our work, acknowledging that we are co-creators with God. In his book titled *Creativity*, Matthew Fox has this to say:

> Let us not deceive ourselves or live in a silly illusion about our creativity. Creativity is a choice. (In theological terms, it is grace and works operating together. It is an option to live a life with grace.) Creativity is not a particular gift given to certain people only. It is a personal choice and a cultural choice. An individual choice and a family, professional, and societal choice, and at this time in our history it is a species choice. We choose whether to let creativity flow or not—in our educational systems, our media, our politics, our economics, our religions, our very psyches. In theological terms, it is a matter of letting the Spirit in, the Christ in, the Buddha nature in.

It is time to let the Spirit in. It is time to teach without fear. You know the arguments against creativity, I'm sure:

This is too childish. Doesn't Jesus call us to be child-like?

The kids are too sophisticated. In nearly thirty years of teaching, I have yet to find a group of children or teens who have been too sophisticated.

What if I fail? Much can be learned from failure; in so many instances, what our human minds deem as failure is often a success.

Things are too noisy. My grandfather had a good reply for this one. He said, "You'll have enough time to be quiet in the grave."

There's not enough Scripture in this. Scripture might not be in everything you do, but if faith runs through what you teach and how you teach it, connections will be made.

It's much too risky. And if you don't take that risk, how will you know what you can do?

We have to let go of old habits. As Jesus said, you can't put new wine into old wineskins. Only people who are not in touch with their creativity, with their grace, have no desire to do anything differently.

Creative people are committed to risk and are always willing to walk into the darkness: this is where we must dare to go. We can see what's in the light. But in order to find new ways of seeing, of being, and of teaching our faith, we must delve into the darkness of the unknown.

Creativity is finding out what about you is unique, and discovering a way to express that uniqueness in all parts of your life. Creativity is the natural order of life, the gift of God to us.

As you try to incorporate creativity and the multiple intelligence into the religious education setting, it is important to be in touch with your own faith. You can only give what you have. If you haven't discovered this, begin the search and teach when you feel you are ready. Make God a part of your life. Don't restrict God to a time and place. Let God go with you into the kitchen, out to the grocery store, into your classroom.

In her book, *Knights of the Square Table*, Mabel Watts tells the story of the kitchen boy, Cadmus, who notices that the knights argue all the time because each wants a place at the head of the table. Each knight has a reason for wanting the head place. Cadmus reflects that the knights are all equally brave and noble and important. He knows it and everyone else knows it, but how could they prove it to the knights?

For two evenings in a row the knights don't eat dinner because they refuse to sit anywhere but at the head of the table. The second night Cadmus stays awake, watching the moon. He sees its roundness and thinks about how squares can become round. The next morning, Cadmus and the other kitchen helpers cut off the corners of the table and sand it into a smooth round table.

When the knights arrive that night for dinner, they see the change and realize that there is no head, so no one is more important than the others. They eat together that night and so give birth to the Knights of the Round Table.

This is what we are called to be—members of the round table of the Lord, each of us offering our best, using all of our intelligences so all believers realize what can be possible when we take a leap of faith and trust in the Spirit.

I wish you happy wandering through the creative world of multiple intelligences!

Resources

Bellanca, James. *Active Learning Handbook for the Multiple Intelligence Classroom.* Arlington Heights, Illinois: IRI/Skylight, 1997.

Berryman, Jerome W. *Godly Play.* San Francisco: Harper San Francisco, 1991.

Doyle, Brendan. *Julian of Norwich.* Santa Fe, New Mexico: Bear & Company, 1983.

Fox, Matthew. *Creativity.* New York: Jeremy P. Tarcher/Putnam, 2002.

Gardner, Howard. *Frames of Mind.* New York: Basic Books, 1983.

———. *Multiple Intelligence: The Theory in Practice.* New York: Basic Books, 1993.

Larson, Roland S. and Doris E. *Values and Faith.* Minneapolis, MN: Winston Press, 1976.

McCarroll, Tolbert. *Guiding God's Children.* Mahwah, NJ: Paulist Press, 1983.

Nicholson-Nelson, Kristen. *Developing Students' Multiple Intelligence.* New York: Scholastic Professional Books, 1998.

Peet, Bill. *Cowardly Clyde.* Boston: Houghton-Mifflin, Co., 1979.

Shaffer, Carolyn and Kristin Anundsen. *Creating Community Anywhere.* New York: G.P. Putnam & Sons, 1993.

Shulevitz, Uri. *The Treasure* (adapted from an English tale). New York: Farrar-Straus-Giroux, 1978.

Varga, Judy. *The Magic Wall.* New York: William Morrow and Co., 1970.

Watts, Mabel. *Knights of the Square Table.* New York: Lantern Press, 1973.

Of Related Interest

Prayer and Multiple Intelligences
Who I Am Is How I Pray
BERNADETTE STANKARD

Each of us chooses a different path in our search for a deep relationship with God. Some find joy in sacred music or dance. Others prefer silence and meditation. Throughout history the approaches to prayer have been as many and varied as those who undertake the spiritual journey. The one constant, though, has been that all the paths spring from the multiple intelligences people possess and through which they learn and communicate best. In clear, insightful prose, rich with real-life examples, Bernadette Stankard discusses these intelligences and how they enable us to pray "as we are" and so develop a deeper friendship and intimacy with God whose love transforms us.

$12.95 | 120 pages | 1-58595-512-1

What Do You Know?
A Catholic Identity Game for the Whole Community
PEGGY O'NEILL FISHER

The twenty-seven intergenerational identity games in this book focuses on learning more about our faith, particularly through our liturgical seasons and experiences. The questions range from easy to challenging and can be used as icebreakers, for review of content already learned, as discussion starters, to share basic information, and for sacrament preparation. The process is informative and enjoyable and through it the whole parish community will share lively discussion and renewed interest in the Catholic faith.

$14.95 | 80 pages | 1-58595-586-2

To Walk Humbly
Stories and Activities for Teaching Compassion and Justice
For Ages Ten through Thirteen
ANNE E. NEUBERGER

Here Anne Neuberger offers fifty-five wonderful stories from around the world to help young Catholics "connect" with the social, environmental, and economic problems of children around the globe. It encourages them to accept and think of these children as family, as sisters and brothers. Story topics include school life, child labor, cultural and religious celebrations, hunger, racism, poverty, sharing, generosity, and lifestyles. Recommended for faith formation sessions, confirmation preparation, religion class, retreats, and intergenerational gatherings.

$19.95 | 144 pages | 1-58595-616-6

TWENTY THIRD 23rd
PUBLICATIONS
PO Box 6015 • New London, CT 06320
www.23rdpublications.com